Divorce Diva

Marci Darling

HOUSE OF MARTINI

Divorce Diva

Cover Design

Cover Art 2020 © Paul Dexter Inigo

Formatting by Rik: <u>Wild Seas Formatting</u>
(http://WildSeasFormatting.com)

Print: ISBN: 978-0-9981362-4-0 ($9.99)
Ebook: ISBN: 978-0-9981362-5-7 ($5.99)

Library of Congress Control Number: 2020923169

Praise for Miss Marci Darling

Fast paced and fun, *Martini Mystery* is a great read from Marci Darling, who shares my passion for burlesque, the circus, and New Orleans. It was a delight reading about so many places I've haunted in New Orleans.

> -- Leslie Zemeckis, Bestselling Author of *Goddess of Love Incarnate: The Life and Times of Stripteuse Lili St. Cyr* and *Behind the Burly Q: The Story of Burlesque in America*

This is a tremendously fun, high-spirited read that is one part mystery, one part history of esoteric New Orleans history, and a couple of dashes of fashion. After a strange encounter at a nighttime parade, Darling takes readers on a wild trip through New Orleans secret societies and local lore in a dash to solve the mystery of a dead man, a mysterious key, an antique photograph, and a seemingly cursed Grace Kelly purse. She writes with wit and breeze and puts a smile on the reader's face, even when dastardly deeds are afoot.

> -- Keith Allison, NYU Senior Editor, Author of *Cocktails & Capers: Cult Cinema, Cocktails, Crime, and Cool*

How can a book be both dark and mysterious yet imbued with fun and frivolity? *Martini Mystery* does just that, sweeping readers into an immersive and lushly evocative New Orleans adventure.

> -- Michelle Finamore, Author of *Hollywood Before Glamour: Fashion in American Silent Film* and *Brioni: The Man Who Was (Classics)*

Martini Mystery is a fabulous escapade into the glamour of New Orleans, its mysterious nightlife, costumes, and ominous undertones. A page-turning mystery that will also give you glittering giggles.

-- Shannon Kirk, International Bestselling author of *Method 15/33, In the Vines, Gretchen, The Extraordinary Journey of Vivenne Marshall*

Martini Mystery is a fun read and perfect for a book club. You can serve food typical of New Orleans dishes along with the cocktails that were listed in the book.

-- Megan O'Block, Bestselling Author of *Heart to Table, Diamonds and Dishes, Metamorphosis*

Author Marci Darling strikes a delightful balance with charming and provocative characters while providing a seriously suspenseful game of cat and mouse. With charming wit and dramatic flare, Darling dishes up opulence, cloak and dagger in one heaping serving. *Martini Mystery* is a captivating and truly satisfying first novel by Marci Darling.

-- Leslie Martini, Author of *Matilda, the Algonquin Cat*

Table of Contents

Dear Divas,

I started writing Divorce Diva as a heartbroken, traumatized terrified wife and mother, and ended it as a ferociously empowered single mom love goddess living in sparkling joy at my optimal potential and happier than I ever thought possible. How did I get here? What did I learn along the way? How did I heal my broken heart? I will tell you how: writing. My pen was my portal to process my pain.

The city of my marriage was burnt to the ground, and writing allowed me to create a new kingdom for my new family of three: me and my children. It was scary as hell to put my stories out into the world, but here they are. I believe they are best read at random, in a bubble bath with a box of chocolates next to you and perhaps some Ella Fitzgerald or Eartha Kitt playing on your record player. At least that's how I like to read. Writing my truth is how I survived and flourished, and now you hold my stories in your hands. I hope they fill you with hope, humor, and chutzpah.

Cheers!

Marci Darling

To all my broken-hearted beloveds
May peace cup your hearts and hold them gently
So you remember you are the Bees Knees
And you can sashay back out into the world at your
optimal power with sparkle and panache!

Chapter 1
My First Morning As A Divorcee…

(Written while wearing a massive feathered hat as befitting a Divorcee)

It's a strange feeling. Yesterday I was a married woman in the midst of a brutal divorce fight with all of my energy going into defending and protecting my children and myself.

Today I am a single Mom.

It feels surreal, like I'm walking on the battlefield after the battle, surrounded by carnage, the sounds of gunshots and clink of swords echoing around me. I'm covered in the blood and wounds of battle, and looking around at all the broken dreams and hopes around me, and my ears are muffled from the new silence after being assaulted over and over again by the war. We've been battling for so long. Is it really over? Or will he come back swinging for a surprise attack? Am I still standing? Am I still whole? Do I have wounds that are tearing me apart that I can't see? I look at my hands, my arms, scan my body in slow motion.

Am I okay?

Yesterday in court, the judge sent us out of the room, over and over, to change wording in our agreement. After four hours of this, I sat down next to my ex and finally laid my head on his shoulder. Even with all the betrayal and pain, he always had a good shoulder for my head. He put his arm around me and we sat, watching the judge, and the bailiff, and the movements around the courtroom, like we were in a movie. He whispered,

"If only you had let me be a little more me." I whispered back, "If only you didn't have a wandering weiner."

We snickered like we were in 7th grade and not two full-fledged grown-ups.

Finally, the judge looked at both of us and said, "An irretrievable breakdown of your marriage occurred and you agree that there is no hope of putting it back together?"

(Well, she said something like this.)

He said "Yes."

I said "Yes as the tears bubbled up."

Then she said, "I hereby grant your divorce."

Like a Fairy godmother granting wishes, except she's granting the worst wish ever—divorce and all the pain that goes with it.

If marriage represents two souls leaping into life together, with great love and devotion, with the brightest of hope that they will walk by each other's sides, be loyal and faithful to each other, grow old together, and take care of each other—divorce is the opposite.

Divorce is despair, hopelessness, darkness and deep sadness.

The great dream is officially over.

I never thought in a million years that I would ever end up married. I was happy being a glamorous aunt to my nieces and nephews, and I never wanted to depend on a man. This was partly because I was happy as I was, and partly because my worst fear was being abandoned. I didn't want to give my heart and soul to someone which I consider treasures, only to have him throw it all on the ground and stomp on it.

And I never thought in a million years I would end up divorced.

My heart and soul were thrown down and lit on fire.

So I'm taking them back.

All these years, I had a sign over my front door that said, Fairy Tales Do Come True because my husband and children were my fairy tale. I couldn't believe I had created something so beautiful, and for me, rare and precious. The three of them were my pinnacle in life, and I thought if I never do anything else with my life, it's okay because I have this.

I threw the sign out in the trash after that horrible morning when it all fell apart.

And now it's the next morning, and I'm walking in slow motion among the carnage. It will take some time to take it all in.

I woke up this morning and ordered a new sign to put over my door.

Fairy Tales Do Come True.

I'm rewriting the fairy tale.

No sleeping princesses here. I'm awake.

No dwarves to mine for jewels for me. I'm doing the mining myself.

No bluebirds to do my dishes. I'm doing it myself.

If the castle was surrounded by thorns during divorce, they are now cut away, replaced by buds and blooms so beautiful I want to weep.

No prince is galloping in to rescue us.

But we don't need rescuing, because I am here.

The only galloping and rescuing being done around here is being done by me.

And guess what?

For this one moment, I'm not afraid.

And so I invite blooming flowers and singing bluebirds into my home along with generosity and abundance, love, light and laughter, harmony and peace, justice and fairness, integrity and honesty and clarity...

Oh my goddess!

I can now have a home filled with these things that are so important to me.

The darkness is gone.

I can't believe it.

As Anais Nin said so beautifully, "Last night I wept. I wept because the process by which I have become a woman was painful. I wept because I was no longer a child with a child's blind faith. I wept because my eyes were opened to reality... I wept because I could not believe any longer and I love to believe. I can still love passionately without believing. That means I love humanly. **I wept because I had lost my pain and I am not yet accustomed to its absence.**"

And for the record, I still believe.

Chapter 2
How Coaching a 6th Grade Football Team Helped This Glamour Girl Cope with Death and Divorce

As so often happens in life, I have ended up in many situations I never dreamed I'd be in: dancing on tour with the Go-Go's; riding a Vespa across a stage while Placido Domingo sings my favorite aria; belly dancing in the bush with a native tribe in Kenya; go-go dancing on a box with a ten-foot tall lobster with the B-52's next to me singing Rock Lobster; opening for Paul McCartney dressed like a princess; graduating from Harvard; so today when I stood on the football field at the local elementary school coaching my 12-year-old son's flag football game, and that surreal feeling of "Whoes life am I living?" came over me, I did what I do best: I buckled in and went on the ride.

A year ago, two doozy hits took me down for the count: my beloved father moved in with me so I could get him proper medical care, and within six very intense weeks of doctor visits saying "Yes we can get him better," and "No, there's nothing we can do"; 2am ambulance calls; and finally landing in a hospice where the ravages of cancer twisted us all to a new level of suffering, I was putting Vaseline on his lips as he took his last breath.

My heart truly and deeply broke.

Three weeks later, my son was sleeping in my bed because he was having nightmares. At 5am I crawled up the stairs to snuggle with my husband, who was sleeping in my son's bed, only to find him on his ipad, which he quickly hid from me. He tried to lie his way out of it, but he finally admitted he had been having an affair for a long time. "You're in love?" I asked him. He laughed and said, "No." Then he ran out the door, with my 13-year-old daughter screaming from deep in her guts at him, "Don't leave!!!!!!!!!"

Sixteen years together, two children, twelve years of a sexy romantic marriage, cheering for him every step of the way, and somehow I missed that my husband was living a double life. I thought he adored me, cherished me, and loved me deeply.

I was completely blindsided, and my ability to believe in fantasy apparently overrode reality and truth.

I keep thinking he's going to kiss me on the forehead and wake me up, and my father will be here and my kids won't be suffering, and this will have all been a terrible nightmare.

In a cruel ironic twist, he teaches Ethics at a college in Boston. Fucking Ethics. If it wasn't so heartbreaking, it would be hilarious.

So here I am, 49 years old, on the football field in late October in New England, orange leaves swirling around me, a cool wind whipping my hair, and a gang of 12-year-old boys looking to me for guidance.

I had no intention of coaching anything *ever*. In fact, I have found coaches in general to be a loud and rowdy bunch. I'm not a sports person, I'm a glamourpuss, more comfortable in a pink petticoat with bright red lipstick that matches my perfectly manicured nails. I've never played football, and I don't even like to watch it unless my son is playing. Even then, the struggle is real.

But the team couldn't happen without a volunteer coach, so I volunteered and took a crash course in the rules, watching Youtube tutorials and asking questions.

What's an endzone?

From here to here.

(I scratch my head.) So, you're saying if they get between these two lines they score points, yes?

(Now they scratch their heads.)

The ref asks me if we want to punt. I don't know what a punt is, although it sounds kind of dirty. I glance at my team, they all nod so I say yes, we want to punt. And later I'll ask everyone I know to explain a punt to me, and I'm still not clear on it. After a touchdown where I'm screaming the loudest as my little guy races down the field, the ref says 1 or 2? I have no idea what he's talking about, so I always say 2, since 2 is more than 1. I'm still not exactly sure what that means, although I now know its points. I have two other moms coaching with me, and they have learned on the fly with me, although they seem to know more than I do. At least they *dress* sporty, so they *must* know more than I do. I run along the sidelines in my floppy sun hats, giant sunglasses, my retro dress with the apples on it and a petticoat underneath, and my Gucci sneakers that are covered in rainbow sparkles that say "LOVED."

They're sneakers: they count as sporty-ish.

I like to remind myself that I am loved, even when I feel that I'm not.

And guess what? We've won enough games to put us in first place. Last week we defeated the undefeated team in the league.

But today, well today, we got crushed. The other team made four immediate touchdowns. Four! Negativity cloaked our team in clouds darker than the lurking rain clouds overhead. One boy quit trying. One started complaining. Two had their arms over their heads saying, "We're getting crushed. It's over." And one started crying.

I called them together. "Guys, listen up. There is *no* complaining and *no* negativity. That's bad sportsmanship." I searched my brain for something they could relate to. "Do you think Black Panther started complaining when the bad guys had him pinned down under his foot and he was covered in dirt and blood and in pain? Do you think he started crying and saying, "It's over"? NO! He got up and tried harder with laser focus and he beat the villain! We can still beat them!"

I wasn't sure they were buying my speech, but they had stopped panicking and were watching me, so I kept going. "Look, I went to my first Patriots game last weekend. I was trying to get some tips and at half time it was 24 to nothing *for the other team*. The Pats were *losing*. Did they come out crying and saying we're crushed? NO! They came back out with MORE FOCUS, and tried even harder, and they won. If I see any of you out there not trying, I will take you off the field and replace you with someone who cares. If we go down, we will go down fighting! We can do this, and even if we don't win, we will play our best and hardest until the very last second. Let's do this."

They all stared at me.

My voice was hoarse from yelling, but we played the second half, made three touchdowns, and even though the other team made another one, we stopped them from making a few more.

I ran up and down the sidelines, cheering my kids on, taking out anyone who quit trying and replacing them with a player who wanted it, until the first player was ready to come back in. We lost, but we went down fighting. In the end, I gathered them together and told them, "You did a great job because you DIDN'T GIVE UP! You tried harder. That's what you do. Life will crush you, because that's what life does in between the magical moments, but *you don't lay down*, you get up and you crush *it!*"

And I came home, hoarse and jubilant that they made it through.

Then I realized, I need to coach myself. How many times a day in the past year did I cry 'Uncle'? Doubled over and sobbing on the floor, I'd cry, "Life, you win, you've done it, you've crushed me, I'm done." Sobbing, heartbroken, bereft, griefstricken, I'd fall to my knees feeling like my heart was going to just stop. Well, guess what? I always managed to stand back up. And I'm doing more than just standing, I'm dancing, twirling my sadness into art, turning my "wailing into dancing" as my favorite Psalm says. Well, it's the only Psalm I know, and if you're going to know one Psalm, it's a beauty.

When people ask me how I'm doing, I say, "I'm steering the ship. There's nobody else now, just me, and the kids are on the ship and it is not going down, not with me at the wheel."

In my mind, our beautiful ship looks like a pirate ship sailing through warm starry skies, with me at the battered wooden wheel, the wind in the kids' hair and a rainbow sail lit by moonlight. My brother always tells me, "Stay the course, you're doing great." I love that image of the three of us, me and the kids, staying the course, steering towards the North Star, in warm starlit skies.

On our Flag Football team, our secret code name for our Hail Mary play is "On Your Knees." I didn't know football had secret codes! I love secret codes! That means everyone runs to anywhere that's open, turns to catch the ball, and makes the touchdown. In this play, anything is possible, miracles are possible, even the slowest fumbling kid can score-- you just have to get open. Life hasn't crushed me, because I'm open, open to the next adventure, steering the ship, staying the course, strong and steady, and if my team remembers anything from this year of playing 6th grade flag football, I hope they remember the heartbroken crazy lady coach running down their sidelines in her pink petticoat, yelling at them to get up, focus, and try harder, no matter what, and most importantly, to get open and stay open, because that's how the miracles happen.

Chapter 3
I Have Found the Paradox That If I Love Until It Hurts, Then There Is No More Hurt, Only More Love.
Mother Teresa

I've seen things during my time that there are no words for, and now, at the age of 50, when the amount of loss and trauma in my life is staggering and seems too heavy to bear, guess what makes it lighter? Guess what takes away the sting of betrayal, the stunning pain, the sad and heavy heart?

Serving children.

I just completed my training to become a Wish Fairy for the Make-A-Wish Foundation and I'm over the moon excited to begin granting wishes! Anyone who knows me knows I love children and fairies, and granting wishes, so this is a perfect fit for me!

And I've found over and over again in my life, nothing soothes the soul and heals the heart like service work.

Humility, compassion, care–throughout my life, my volunteer work has always been my form of "church.'

Holding a child with AIDS was my sacred work. When I touched their faces, I felt like I was touching the face of god, or grace, or whatever you want to call that boundless unconditional expansive love.

Through my work, I found that surrounding a soul with love and care had the unknown side effect of surrounding my own soul with boundless love.

How tricky is that?

You would think it would be draining or depleting to go to a shelter to work with sick or homeless children but the secret is– it's actually fulfilling beyond your wildest dreams to hold those children in your arms.

Plus, it's a weekly slap in the face that puts your own life into perspective really fast.

So when it seems like "the shit is hitting the fan," as they say, and it seems my life is falling apart with loss and deep soul trauma, it is time to ramp up the compassion and service, and let the sacred moments work their magic.

As a teenager, some of my most memorable moments were my volunteer experiences working with the Special Olympics or delivering gifts to the State mental hospital children's wing where they let us play with the kids until two of them became violent and were dragged out of the room.

When I turned eighteen, I wanted to be a movie star, a pirate, a princess, a lawyer, or a nun.

I studied Mother Teresa and worked at the Food and Shelter Coalition in Provo, and inquired about what it would take to join the Sisters of Calcutta. The scratchy underwear and no-hot-water thing made me turn elsewhere to fulfill my need to serve.

Back in those days, it wasn't the click of a few buttons to find a way to serve. After I moved to Hollywood, I went to the United Way's offices and walked up the dark dank stairway with the smell of mildew wafting through the air, and into an office where a small man in glasses thumbed through dog-eared index cards to find me a position. He sent me to Daybreak, a shelter for mentally ill homeless women, but when one of the volunteers had her hair lit on fire by a resident, and the place closed down, I went back to the office and told the man I wanted to work with children. He then called CBA.

CBA, Caring for Babies with AIDS, was a residential shelter in LA where I volunteered weekly for ten years. I did everything from reading stories to washing dishes, to playing tag, to rocking newborns to sleep. Some kids stayed there for years. Others were in and out in a couple of weeks. When I arrived, CBA had two little houses side by side with a yard between them. Disney animators had volunteered to come in and paint murals over the walls. We initially had children 0-6, but as protease inhibitors came out and the survival rate went up, our kids grew into teenagers. I created a Creative Dance Therapy for the kids and it was incredible to watch their transformation. We re-enacted the *Wizard of Oz*. They LOVED pretending to be whirled around in a tornado and waking up in a magical land. We danced to everything, from Barney to Beyonce, and the kids loved it -- even the teens.

Of course, there were children that were immobile or too sick to dance. For one eight-year-old, who was blind and very very sick from the disease, I would go into his room, caress his head or hold his hand, and sing softly to him. For four-year-old Raven, who couldn't move below her neck, she would sit propped up by pillows as I sang "Miss Polly had a Dolly" or "What if All the Raindrops were Lemon Drops and Gumdrops?" and she would smile and laugh, watching me with big brown eyes and gorgeous long lashes.

Music and dance gave them time to be kids again–to forget about hospital visits and endless meds, drug addict parents and siblings who didn't survive.

Raven was at the shelter for a few years, and on so many meds, that finally they decided to take her off them. I showed up and no one was in the room with her. They made me wear a gown and a mask, before I went in to stand next to her crib, put my hand on her heart, just like I'd seen Mother Teresa do in pictures. I sang softly to her, all her favorite songs. She couldn't see my face because of the mask, but she could see my eyes, and there was so much love in that room. She looked terrified, but seemed comforted a little bit by my presence and the songs... It was hard as hell to not fall on the floor sobbing, but I stayed with her as her lungs filled with fluid and she took her last breaths.

My mother cried when I told her about Raven. She shook her head and said, "I'm too sensitive. I could never do that job. How can you do it?"

A better question for me is, "How can you not?"

I went to too many funerals during those years with tiny caskets and balloons, and every time I thought, "this is too much, I need a break," another child would show up like Gloria.

Gloria showed up with patches of missing hair and eyes that could barely open. She was four, but couldn't walk. When I held her it was like holding a feather. I circled my fingers around her tiny tiny wrist, and sang softly to her. She vomited on my shoes and I gently cleaned her up, knowing I was not going to take a break.

That's how I ended up there for ten years.

Over the last several years, while raising my own children, I have volunteered all over the place, with teenagers who had cancer in the New Orleans hospital, (I still have "Kung Fu Fighter" ringing in my head all these years later after competing with the teens, playing it over and over again on guitar–video game style–they always beat me.) I have volunteered at schools and museums, and spent the last five years at Horizons for Homeless Children at shelters around Boston.

Through it all, I've been endlessly inspired by another unknown side effect of service work–the other volunteers. There are armies of people out there quietly doing volunteer work, unsung heroes from every walk of life who show up and help, who raise their hand when someone says they need help. I love these people. I am inspired and amazed by them.

And another thing I learned, that I have found so very very important as I go through my own staggering heartbreaks and loss: I learned to let go. The children showed up at CBA, and I didn't know if I would be loving them for a few hours, a few years, or many many years. I had to be okay with that, just love them for this eternal moment, "a handprint on my heart" as the song says. I will love and love and love over and over, knowing it may only last a day, or an hour, or a hundred years, but I'll still love just the same.

More tricks–the more I love, the more I am filled with love. How does that happen? I don't know, it's mystical, and I'm okay with the mystery.

I'll just keep loving.

And over and over again, I so deeply resonate with Mother Teresa's quote: "I have found the paradox that if I love until it hurts, then there is no more hurt, only more love."

Chapter 4
Revenge Body

So my current revenge body is shaped more like a marshmallow than an hourglass.

There's an angel and devil on each of my shoulders—except one is a couch potato and one is Wonder Woman.

This is the story of the endless battle between my inner Couch Potato and my Inner Wonder Woman.

Here is a battle sample:

I come home after an insanely stressful day in divorce court. I haven't slept in days, my brain feels like it's on fire, my heart is broken, and I have a migraine on the periphery, threatening to throw gasoline on the fire that is already in my brain.

WW: Great idea: you should go work out. You will feel so much better afterwards. Play your favorite songs, get your heart pumping, your blood flowing, let's do this!

CP: Marciiiiii!!! Work out? Have you lost your mind? You will feel better if you come lay on the Love Sac, so cozy, so comfy. Come veg! Come binge watch something! You deserve it! You've had a rough day!! I'll support you!!

WW: You will feel terrible after laying around! Like a Jet-puffed marshmallow. Come work out! You will clear your mind, get toned, rock on! No excuses! Let's do it!

CP: Girrrrrl!! One workout isn't going to do anything for you. Plus it will stink in there. You will run into people, you will have to talk. Don't stress! Treat yourself! Get an ice cold Diet Coke, pop some popcorn, grab some Hot Tamales, some Cinnamon Bears... Get cuddly under the pink blanket and watch an amazing story play out! You are so lucky to be living in the Golden Age of TV and Movies all at your fingertips. Touch the remote and you can watch whatever your heart desires! You deserve it! It will smell good, you won't have to talk to anyone... Maybe you'll even get inspired to write your own hit tv show! That's it! It's actually *research*, not vegging!! Come on!

WW: (wrestling CP behind her so she can be heard) Girrrl!! You will feel terrible if you lay down! Hours will pass and you haven't moved! Like Jabba the Hut! Eat those cinnamon bears and you will be shaped like one! Get your ass to the gym!

CP: Work out tomorrow. Tonight is your Farewell to Fat party — time to chill.

WW: At least take a walk around the block with the dog. Smell the trees, let the starlight dance in your hair, get your blood flowing a little.

CP: (Sigh) I will allow a 15 minute walk, but if you get up there and don't feel like it, turn right around. Come lay on me! I'll be waiting!

For many reasons:

1. Baking is a stress reliever for me, therefore I do a lot of it. I love measuring things, putting them into a bowl and creating something delicious.

2. The *smell* of baking is a stress reliever for me. The smell of chocolate chip cookies baking is soothing to the soul, at least my soul. I love the warmth of the kitchen, the smell of baking bread, cookies, or something delicious. For the kids, it provides security — they love knowing where Mom is, they love the house smelling like baking bread or muffins or cookies, and they congregate in the kitchen while I bake to do their homework, read, draw, or dance. Baking is something you can do while you are talking, so I can pay attention to them AND my muffins at the same time. In New Orleans, the local children called me The Cookie Lady because I was always passing out cookies.

3. When I was a Waldorf preschool teacher, baking was encouraged every day. Waldorf philosophy believes that it is nourishing to the human soul to mix dough, knead it, place it on warm windowsill to rise, knead it again, then bake it. So we started out every school morning by baking bread. Our classroom smelled incredible, and the warmth of the oven on a snowy day provided a hearth for the kids to play. In Italian, they call the hearth "Focolare" which is where the word "Focus" comes from, and it makes sense that the hearth, the fire, the oven, the smells, provide a sense of security and nourishment for the human brain. If the fire is lit, the room is warm and smells like food, you know you are okay for this moment — you aren't running from danger or a threat. So on a physiological level, you are safe.

4. It's soothing to adults too. Even in Hollywood when I lived in the Royal Palace, I would bake cookies and my friends would sit in our royal blue kitchen with me, (with Kim's red coca cola signs and a darling little refrigerator from the 1950's that we bought downtown for $30 because it was cheap and cute and round. It leaked, and got all our food wet and was never very cold, but hey, it was cute). We'd tell stories and double over laughing, while I baked and passed out cookies, even though everyone was always on diets.

5. Is there anything better than sneaking a little cookie dough as sheets go into the oven? I love the taste of warm cookies straight from the oven, they melt in your mouth and it wouldn't be a stretch to say they are a little orgasmic. In fact, I'm not ashamed to say that when my ex and I got romantic, instead of "talking dirty" I would have him read me dessert menus. Try it. You're welcome.

6. Baking is not good, however, for a gorgeous strong healthy body. Neither is cookie dough. My sister-in-law relieves her stress by working out and it has really worked well for her. Not only does she have a rockin' body, but after 5 kids, two divorces, and losing some very close loved ones, she's become a fitness professional, winning competitions and

rocking the tiniest pink bikini you've ever seen. And she's over 40. She's my inspiration. I cheer her on from my kitchen, taking trays of warm cookies from the oven, while she struts around the stage, her muscles rippling.

7. Sigh.

8. I think I should make working out my stress reliever instead of baking.

9. But here are my excuses. #1: Baking smells better than gym equipment #2: A platter of warm cookies is prettier than a treadmill #3: I can rock an adorable apron better than a pair of leggings #4: The kids love having platters of warm muffins and cookies on the kitchen counter and I love having parades of kids walk by grabbing handfuls. I like to have the teenagers here at my house so I can keep an eye on them and they're not roaming the streets or at other people's houses. Muffins help me attract them.

10. But I do reprimand myself for my excuses and then I take Professor Bananas out on a walk. My favorite walk is after it rains when the sidewalks smell like wet pine trees, the ocean is a little wild, the trees are shimmering with raindrops, the sun hitting the water makes it look like diamonds are falling out of the air.

11. Also, I actually do love to exercise. I love walking on the beach. I love teaching belly dance. I love riding my bike. I love yoga.

After my ex left, I was so distressed I couldn't eat. I lost my sense of taste, and all food tasted disgusting to me, even cookies.

My weight dropped, a pleasant side effect of tragedy — try the Divorce Diet!!

(No don't, it's the worst.)

Kim came to me and made me soup and I couldn't even eat that. Food tasted bitter. Kim was a therapist, and she told me that when a person is traumatized and under extreme stress, the fight or flight instinct appears, our bodies go into overdrive, adrenaline starts shooting through the system at weird times, and it can affect the senses.

I had always weighed around 120-130 most of my adult life, but once I got pregnant with my second child, it was game over. I gained over 75 pounds with his pregnancy even though I was eating the same and exercising. He was well worth the destruction of my body, and if you held up my boy and my rockin body, I'd choose my boy every time.

But I do fantasize about having both—a body I feel good in and my boy. Sigh. Wouldn't it be nice if I could go back to eating whatever I wanted and stay the same size? Now, in order to lose weight, I have to starve myself famine-style. Within a few days, I start to feel so deprived that all hell breaks loose in my mind. All my bouncing pink unicorns turn to snorting raging black horses, the nightmare kind. I become a bad person, a grouchy person, a bad parent, a bad friend, and I no longer have anything nice to say about the world. (Now you know, if I'm ever grouchy, feed me. I'm the opposite of a gremlin—don't feed them after midnight, but for me, feed me at all hours or I become a gremlin). Once Kim and I went on a heart-surgery-patient soup diet together. We spent $70 we didn't have on vegetables and came home and made a huge pot of soup that we planned to eat for the next ten days—only the soup—nothing else. After two bowls, things took a turn for the worst. We had a performance at a nightclub in Malibu and then we drove out to Westlake Village to see my sister. She had m&m's set out in a bowl and I swear they were actually talking, calling my name. I looked in my nephew's frog aquarium and wondered why there was a large delicious brownie in the middle of it. I rubbed my eyes and on second look, it wasn't a brownie, it was a rock.

Now I was hallucinating.

We decided this was crazy, forget it. It was now 9pm, and we drove straight to our favorite Italian restaurant, Miceli's, with the murals on the wall, the wine bottles hanging from the ceiling, the waiters breaking into operatic arias at random times. We had been on our soup diet for 7 hours. We went to Miceli's and ate like we hadn't eaten in seven weeks. We buttered up hot rolls and ate those, followed by pasta smothered in cheese. We were gleeful as we ate, and when we got back to our Royal Palace, we took the soup out of the fridge and dumped it. We never wanted to see it again.

Also, I'm a writer, which is sedentary, an unpleasant side effect of the glory of writing.

So my current revenge body is shaped more like a marshmallow than a toned athlete.

If my ex loved marshmallows, he would LOOOOVE me, and the revenge body would be mine. But all my ex eats is sardines or some form of raw fish, because he's always on his own diet. In fact, he went on a sardine-only diet right as he started falling apart, and I attributed his weird behavior to lack of real food. He was starving his brain, and it made him crazy. I still stand by this. I've seen many good people taken down by starving themselves.

Also, I'm 50, so there are new unusual things happening to my body as it shifts around with the passing years. For example, bat wings. I've always had naturally toned arms. Now, I hold my arms out to the side and with a little twist of my hands, the skin under my biceps starts to quiver. WTF? I noticed this in the mirror one day and thought, huh, is that unbecoming or super cool? I used to watch the lady at church lead the music with a stick, but I never watched the stick, I was too busy watching the flabs of skin under her arms swing back and forth. I didn't find it disgusting, more just interesting. I now have those swinging bat wings, and I've decided to bring them into fashion, so now I declare: Toned arms are out! Bat Wings are In! Also, a few more things I'm bringing into style: Cellulite is gorgeous!! If you are unlucky enough not to have any cellulite, come to my house and I'll give you some cookies so you can have some cellulite of your own!

Muffin Tops? Sizzling and sexy! The more rounder the rolls the better!

Jiggly? I love it!

Chapter 5
Increase what you love: Release what you don't.

One thing I have learned walking through this wild scary forest called Divorce, is that I can handle anything thrown my way, **as long as I stay in my lane**.

What is my lane?

My lane is beauty and magic and generosity. My lane is love and light and laughter and abundance. It's gorgeous, splashed in sunlight or shimmering in moonlight. There are waterfalls and flowers blooming, hopping baby bunnies with big paws and floppy ears, and fluffy kittens sitting calmly with starlight in their whiskers. Sometimes I'm driving through a pink marshmallow world with bouncing rainbow unicorns, glittering mermaids sitting on rocks, combing their hair, and fairies taking baths in the dew drops of flowers.

But when it comes to divorce, I sometimes have to drive through other people's towns, which look a lot like lawyer's offices with white boards and conference rooms and the only good part — candy jars.

Other towns look like dusty offices of overworked therapists with dusty fake flowers in vases, sticky magazines(why???), and dirty coffee cups laying around.

The scariest towns I drive through look exactly like courthouses, where everything is wood, there are flags and state seals, and everyone is extremely serious and your entire life hinges on whether your judge is feeling irritable, hangry, or joyful that day.

(Guess which adjective I've never seen on the face of a judge?)

But I've found, that if I can just stay in my lane, no easy task when people and circumstances are playing chicken, trying to make me swerve, switch lanes, or the worst—run me off my road completely.

It takes focus and hourly practice.

It takes this: Increase What You Love, Release What You Don't.

Divorce brings out the worst in people. Before my awesome car analogy, I described it to my sisters like this: I feel like I am a villager in an ancient settlement in the forest, and there is growling all around me and glowing red eyes in the trees. I am standing in the middle of the village with a wooden a stick to defend myself and my kids, and I don't know where the next attack is coming from, so I spin around and around on high alert, shaking my stick, trying to figure out how I will protect my family.

Psychologists call it hypervigilance and it wreaks all sorts of havoc with your body, like panic attacks, inability to sleep or eat, and feeling like you're having a heart attack.

When I had my first panic attack, I thought I was having a heart attack. I wasn't even thinking. I was driving the kids to school feeling perfectly happy when all of a sudden I couldn't breathe. My chest felt like it was squeezing. I had to pull over, get out of the car and hunch over till I caught my breath. It terrified me and worse, it terrified the kids. My Dr. told me that when a person is under a lot of stress, the body can start shooting out adrenaline at random times, thinking it's in danger and it's time to run. Once I knew that, I could combat the attacks with deep breathing and focusing on something beautiful—a flower, a blade of grass, the light shining through the leaves. Focusing on something beautiful signals to the brain that its not in danger and everything is safe or you wouldn't be looking at the gorgeous yellow swirl on the flower petal. It actually overrides panic and fear and all those very powerful and seemingly uncontrollable negative emotions.

But turns out, they are controllable.

With the divorce, I was out of my element, in a dark and nasty town surrounded by people who were negative, toxic, dishonest, greedy and miserable. My first reaction was outrage. On top of all the trauma the kids and I had been through, the "players" and "aspiring players" (aka meddling in-laws) in the divorce would be trying to cause us further harm.

But then my next response was: I refuse to participate. That isn't my world. And I choose not to live in that world. My world is beauty, love, light, kindness, generosity and abundance.

When I thought of all the "players" up against me and the kids, it felt like I was being slimed by toxic ooze.

When I thought of my world, it felt like I was swimming in joy, a golden waterfall of light with pink blossoms floating around me, beautiful and full of light.

I wrote on an index card: I release all greedy, litigious, dishonest, negative people.

I wrote on a few index cards in bright pink marker: I step into light, love, generosity, abundance, kindness, joy, beauty, and magic.

I taped the "Release" card in the corner of my bathroom mirror and put the "Increase" card front and center so I was seeing it all the time.

My therapist had once told me that you could help rewire your brain from trauma by thinking of some symbol that makes you feel safe—for me it was a sparkling nest surrounded by flowers next to a sign that said "LOVE." Then she said, anytime the trauma came up, move your eyes up and to the left (like you are looking at something in the upper left corner of a ceiling) and visualize the nest. She said to do it over and over. There is something about moving your eyes that way, with the visualization, that helps to override panic, pushing out the trauma, so it doesn't have power over you and you feel safe. It sounded like hocus pocus, but I did it and it worked!

The trauma caused me pain and panic, the nest soothed me and made me feel safe — it's a no brainer that I should practice focusing on the nest instead. It's much easier to *tell* your brain to do something, than it is to actually *make* it do something. But looking up and to the left works the magic *for* you. At least it did for me.

I put one of my cards in my greenhouse next to a waterfall on a branch of my camellia tree, so if I'm sitting or standing in front of my waterfall, my magic words are up and to the left. They say "Love Light Abundance Generosity Kindness Magic Joy" and incredibly, when I go in there, even for one minute to breathe and look at my waterfall and my words, I immediately feel soothed and empowered.

I'm back in my lane. I have noticed the kids are now doing it on their own. I see torn pieces of paper taped up on their mirrors, scribbles in their school notebooks, words that fill them with strength.

This is a terrifying time! I don't know what the future holds for us. I don't know how I will support them, coming from being a stay-at-home Mom and trying to create a career at the age of 50, with a broken heart and a closet full of crazy hats. There are so many things I love love love to do! And none of them pay. Sigh. But if I stay in my lane, I will figure it out with grace and style. I will drive my sparkly car, wear my crazy hats, and encourage the kids to stay in the lane I have created for all of us.

Will we end up swerving into an alleyway, carjacked, and end up panhandling with torn gloves while singing "It's a Hard Knock Life?"

Maybe, but I hope not. And at this point, that's what I have — hope.

Hope that we can handle anything life throws our way.

Hope that if we stay in our lane, at least we will be filled with light and love while life plays out.

And the more we focus on the light and love, the more it increases, while the other stuff releases.

Increase that you love; Release what you don't.
Stay in your lane.

Chapter 6
Magic Marker Mission Statement

One of the first things we did after my ex left was create a mission statement for the remaining three of us, a verbal picture of how we wanted our home to be.

We had hung magic marker mission statements up in our home for years, but one of us had jumped ship and we needed a new one that put the three of us on the same ship. We were all heartbroken and stunned. I was trying to think of anything and everything I could do to help the three of us focus on light and love, and not on our pain.

We brainstormed together and listed the things that were important to all of us, the things we wanted in our family and our home of three. We wrote:

We three daring explorers of the HAM home- Henry, Annabelle, and Mom do hereby strive for a home full of creativity and kindness, integrity and intellectual curiosity, the freedom to make mistakes and ask for rewinds, music, magic, dance, delight, positive words and actions, books, nature walks, and things that are good for the soul, pillow fighting, jumping on the bed, snuggles, laughter, light, love, love, love, and more LOVE!

And we all signed, it taped it up on our kitchen cabinets where we would see it all the time and read it to each other. Henry was 11 when we wrote it, and he came up with the HAM home, because we had just seen Hamilton on Broadway and he loved that Alexander Hamilton signed his name A. Ham.

When someone loses it occasionally, gets really hangry, or grumpy, or plays a prank on a sibling that goes sideways, we ask for rewinds. It's pretty amazing how it works. We all look at each other, take a deep breath, and carry on like it never happened, and no one has had to ask for a rewind in over a year!

We return to it again and again, whenever we need a tuneup in the form of a good old-fashioned jump-on-the-bed dance party, or a quiet walk in the woods, or just to remember our commitment to each other and to the home we have created. If anyone wants to add anything, it is always open to change as the kids get older and our lives change, but no one has added anything yet, because so far it's been perfect.

Chapter 7
Cleaning Out the Spy Closet

I constantly ask myself:

How can I stay connected to my higher self?

How can I stay in the truest of the truths, love?

How can I let go of the pain and hurt caused by my ex to me and my children? (You hurt me? Okay, it sucks, but I can move on from that. But you hurt my children and it's like Monty Python when he cuts off the knight's arm and says, "It's just a flech wound."

Will there ever come a time when I can see my ex's face and not want to

a. flog him

b. throw up

c. feel like I'm being stabbed in the heart

My dream is that I make my life so incredibly wonderful that I barely remember his name.

So, today I had to call in and cancel teaching because my daughter is on Day 7 of Strep Throat. When parenting a sick child, it's kind of like being in the trenches: you are sick with worry, you don't comb your hair, and you don't get out of your sweats because you are running between your child's sick bed and the kitchen, administering medicine and making healthy food.

In the middle of stress, it's always a good idea to bake some muffins and clean out your closet.

So while my daughter slept, I made my famous pumpkin muffins, and as the smell of melting chocolate and warm pumpkin wafted through the house, I opened the door of the spy closet.

We call it the spy closet because the kids used to play hide and seek inside and there are some really good hiding shelves way up high. Also, we keep our spy stuff in there—invisible ink, flashlights, binoculars, rear view glasses, fingerprinting kits, antique spy phones that are perfect for playing spy, etc.

I'm sure you have a spy closet too, right?

I also keep our many colorful umbrellas in there along with my current teaching bags and supplies, so at any point you will find a cornucopia of feathers, glitter, glue, fairies, flowers, beads, pine cones… you get the idea.

If at any time anything is missing in our house, we say, "Look in the spy closet!" And the missing item usually appears.

So I wonder, can organizing the spy closet help me connect to my higher power? I know who would say Yes: Marie Kondo. She's perfect for those of us struggling to get to the next step of our lives. "Marie! It's dark in here! And messy! A beautiful mess, but still messy!"

She would giggle like a fairy and pat me and tell me to hold each item in my hands. If it didn't spark joy, I should thank it for its use and send it on its way.

Okay.

Maybe cleaning out the spy closet will usher in a new era for beauty and prosperity for us.

I have been wanting to clean it for a year. I usually open the door, look around, feel overwhelmed, then close it and carry on with my day. But today, without thinking too much about it, I dragged everything out, then swept and mopped. Then I organized everything and put a few beautiful items back in.

Hmmm, I don't feel any different.

I'm not sure how cleaning the spy closet helps me stay connected to my highest self, but having a clean organized closet seems like a good first step, doesn't it?

I don't know! All I know is that my dirt pile was gorgeous—full of feathers, jewels, glitter, half-eaten nerf bullets—basically a microcosm of my life.

And I wonder if I can Marie Kondo my mind. If my thought doesn't spark joy, maybe I can give it a hug and sweep it away.

I wonder if I can throw out the painful things my ex did and focus on the good things. I hate to admit it because it hurts, but he really did do a lot of wonderful things. There's a reason I fell in love with him and loved him so dearly for so many years. For example, he stared at me and constantly told me I was the most beautiful woman he had ever seen. He wrote me love songs with titles like, "You Brighten the Corners" and "I'll Keep You Safe If You Keep Me Wild" and sang them to me every Christmas Eve with tears running down his face. He stayed right next to me when I gave birth to our daughter and son and wept when he held them. He opened up beautiful worlds to me like transformative food and wine, and he paid for stuff. That's big. Money has never been my strong suit— well I'm great at spending it, not so great at making it. He loved Christmas as much as I do and wanted it to be as magical as I did. He supported my writing and made me feel magical.

So if I leave out the lying... the cheating... the betrayal... the searing pain... and the dark sickness he brought into our home...

I guess it's not so easy to Marie Kondo your brain. Unless, there's a way to keep the thoughts that spark joy, while still holding the space for the darkness too?

Is there a way to do that?

I remember my professor at UCLA telling us that the mark of a well-adjusted person is someone who can accept the dialectic of life in their mind, and still function. This means holding two diametrically opposed ideas at the same time in your mind and knowing that at any moment either or both can be true.

For example, I call parenting the "cruel dialectic of parenting" meaning, you create these beautiful children guide them through their lives with the sole purpose of letting them go. WHAT? If you do your job well, they leave????

It feels too cruel.

I tend my garden, water my flowers, aerate the soil, nurture them every day, and I have a beautiful garden. I do the same to my children, with the purpose of letting them go. It's so painful, and beautiful, and the essence of all life, right?

Loving and letting go, is like writing in disappearing ink. Write something beautiful and watch it disappear.

Loving and letting go, like getting rid of the rear-view glasses and only wearing forward-view glasses.

Loving and letting go, like opening up my rainbow umbrella and having the wind flip it inside out, before taking it out of my hands.

Loving and letting go, like making a gorgeous fairy that is eaten by the dogs the next day.

Loving and letting go—my Dad's warm gnarled hand in mine.

Loving and letting go—my Mom laughing and gushing to me that she loves Cinderella because the prince reminds her of my father.

Loving and letting go—my best friend, Kim, her huge brown eyes and a loving smile.

Loving and letting go—my marriage, my plans for the rest of my life to sleep next to this man I vowed to love forever and ever.

Loving and letting go—every day when I drop the kids at school and let other adults be their teachers and mentors.

Over and over again.

And is this the lesson in divorce? Loving and letting go?

Can I hold in my mind that my ex is both wonderful and a nightmare? Kind and cruel? Beautiful and ugly? Loving and hateful?

I have to eat a warm pumpkin muffin while I think about this.

I don't know how to do this, but I'm doing it anyway. It's not sparking joy, in fact it's only sadness.

I don't see how this can be, but I *live* how this can be. Because that's the choice, right? To live means to love and let go.

Chapter 8
Courtroom Fashion

One of the worst parts of divorce is the legal part. It's so SERIOUS! With one swing of a gavel, some random judge who doesn't know you, or your family, can make a decision that affects you all forever. That's SCARY!

Ugh!! And all that serious brown! It's a color tragedy in a courtroom! Enchantment, humor, whimsy–are all discouraged in court, and if you try to sneak some in, you will get in trouble.

At least that's what my lawyer tells me. (My lawyer is adorable by the way, with piercing blue eyes, thick dark hair, long thick lashes, and a deep gorgeous voice. You're going to be spending a lot of time with your lawyer, and most of it will be stressful, so I recommend making sure your lawyer is eye candy. I mean, why make everything worse by having your representation be on the plain side?)

I struggle with looking "courtroom respectful," but still feeling like me.

So, when I have a court date coming up, I prep by:

Watching one of the many excellent legal shows on television, from *Drop Dead Diva* to *The Good Wife* to *How To Get Away With Murder*. All shows will give you tips on defending yourself if the need arises, and empower you to do just that. "She who knows the law wins." (My lawyer loves it when I send him bullet points on defending me. Ha! Actually, he probably doesn't love it, but I know me and my marriage the best, so I can point out details he may not know that can be used.)

The one thing court shows won't teach you is what to wear to feel your most empowered, most unshakeable, and most strong.

I love Jane in *Drop Dead Diva*. She tries for cute shoes and a little color in her courtroom wardrobes.

For courtroom fashion inspiration, I also love watching the courtroom scene in *Gentlemen Prefer Blondes* with Jane Russell pretending to be Lorelai, played by Marilyn Monroe. Jane wears a blonde wig and gets on the stand wearing a floor length fur coat. During her testimony, she drops the coat to reveal an adorable leotard/corset dance ensemble with fringe. Then she proceeds to dance around the courtroom while singing, shaking her fringe, and creating a courtroom scene that is fabulous. Now if only court had these kinds of lovely surprises, I would be excited to go! Jane Russell in the Cutest Courtroom Outfit ever!

For real court though, it will work against you to wear a dance outfit. A better guide is to wear an outfit closer to the ones worn by Marilyn Monroe and Jane Russell for their fabulous dance number "Bye Bye Baby". Another excellent sartorial ensemble is the dance number "When Love Goes Wrong" after our heroines have lost everything and can't even afford a cup of coffee. They sing to cheer themselves up, while sitting at a cafe wearing gorgeous suits with crisp collars, silk scarves, and gloves and berets. It makes it clear to me that there's no problem that can't be solved with a good musical number. "When Love Goes Wrong:" put on divine gloves and collars and jaunty beret.

Sometimes I peruse court outfits. This comes up with nothing but tennis outfits. So then I peruse different search words like "vintage glamour" or "glamorous criminals," or *American Hustle* because I love 70's rock glam, and my courtroom ensemble ends up including cat-eye sunglasses and boas, or long leather trenches and unbuttoned shirts. I send my ideas to my best friend, Kim, or to my Martini Club. My Martini Club consists of two fellow Moms, Jacquie and Cristie. We meet once a week for martinis and deep mom chats, which usually swings from kids to elderly parents to potential billion dollar business ideas to furry balls. We pride ourselves on our juvenile humor, and proudly gift each other and laugh hysterically over fluffy balls and martini socks. When one of us calls an Emergency Martini Meeting, we all drop whatever we are doing and meet to discuss the emergency. When they advise me on courtroom ensembles, they say things like, "You should have your ex wear that fringe leotard" or "Maybe tone it down a little?" Or "I would save that for a date night or club night and try something a little more muted." Then I'll send my ensemble ideas to my sisters who send me laughing emojis and are no help at all.

For example, I took my little ones to see *Midsummer Night's Dream* in the woods on Martha's Vineyard, and I somehow got it into my head that fairy outfits were mandatory. We planned our ensembles for days, wore fairy wings and glitter and flower wreaths. When I showed up, the kids pointed out to me that no one else was dressed like fairies. (I hadn't noticed, blinded by all the glitter in my eyelashes.) I sighed. This happens more frequently than I care to admit. (Once I attended a company Christmas party in NYC with my ex, and had decided in my head it was a *Great Gatsby* theme. I spent all day getting ready, wore a champagne sparkly flapper dress with a cabernet velvet 1920's big collar jacket, and walked into the restaurant to a table full of bearded grungy dudes in jeans. Sigh. In any case, the courtroom fashion inspiration in *Legally Blonde* is excellent for research. Elle dresses in bright pink, looks amazing, and still manages to save her innocent client from the clink.

Sometimes I fantasize about being a judge. I don't like the black robe, but I love the idea of everyone standing when I enter the room, and listening to wild stories all day–can you imagine? All the drama? All the storytelling? I'm not equipped to be a judge because I generally believe everything everyone says, and I feel sorry for people, which can work against me when I'm dealing with a scallywag. In my courtroom, I would pass out warm chocolate chip cookies, issue an edict that everyone entering my courtroom must wear feet pajamas, and settle in for some seriously spellbinding storytelling. I suppose I'm better suited to teaching preschool where there are no scallywags, or if there are, they are short enough to be humorous and not distressing. However, I love the idea of exacting justice on the people who have done wrong. I'm just not sure what that justice would be. I was on the Board of the Waldorf School in New Orleans where my daughter went to preschool, and the teachers had a unique way of treating behavioral issues. When a child was acting up, they weren't sent to detention or the principal's office (there was no principal), they were sent into the hallway to knit. Waldorf believes that knitting is therapeutic and calming and that working with your hands in intricate ways forms new neural connections that are healing. But I don't think that would work with thieves and murderers.

In the end, does it really matter what you wear? I say YES!! Even court can be glamorous and fun with the right outfit! Okay, that's not true. It won't be either of those things, but it can be more tolerable with an outfit that makes you feel confident and gorgeous. I don't know about you, but a beautiful pair of shoes, a swing dress in luscious colors, pearls around my neck and flowers in my hair just make me feel GOOD! And there's no more important time to feel good than in a courtroom.

So rock that court outfit!! And send me photos of your ensembles so I can pin them to my wall and cheer you on!

Chapter 9
Sell the Jewels, Take the Trip

When you are thrown screaming into the abyss that is divorce, you may decide to open a window and throw his things out onto the sidewalk, or tear off your pearl necklace and diamond rings and flush them down the toilet like my sister did.

I understand, I truly do.

After I caught my ex cheating, I tried to throw his things out the window, but it was too much and too heavy. So I held my head high while my body shook with sobs and my best friend flew in from across the country to hold me as I called movers to take everything away. Except for all framed photos of him. I had a special plan for those. I took a hammer to them, then threw them on the floor and stomped on them.

And then I thought, what about my jewels? My ex had loved to give me jewels from Tiffany's: a double strand of pearls for my Harvard graduation; diamond and platinum earrings for our first Christmas; unique diamond and platinum engagement and wedding rings; a dripping diamond necklace (that I loved), and a gorgeous halo diamond rings for my 40th birthday. Oh and a triple halo diamond ring which he gave me on his knees after the last time I caught him cheating. He said the three diamonds represented him and the children and his devotion and commitment to remember that he always held our three hearts in his hands. Ha! When I would wear my jewels out on our date nights, he would gaze at me over a bottle of wine, love in his eyes-- at least I thought it was love-- and say, "I like to see you dripping in Tiffany's." Of course who wouldn't want to hear those words? But you can keep your Tiffany's, I prefer honesty, integrity and loyalty.

The jewels seemed cursed now, bad luck, and I didn't want to be reminded of all the lies and broken promises that came with them. I called various dealers and even took a big stack down to a jewelry shop, who offered me $500.00 for all my Tiffany's diamonds and pearls. I was tempted to dump it, but I'm glad I didn't. You'll never guess where I finally sold it all... EBAY!

WHAT?

I know. I had no idea people bought jewels from Ebay, seems awfully risky. But there's a big market on Ebay for Tiffany's jewels. Apparently it's easy to prove their authenticity as each piece is engraved with tiny serial numbers I had never noticed. I was surprised that I was able to sell each piece for a decent amount. I mean, a fraction of the original cost, but I didn't care. I had a plan. It was thrilling when the money rolled in, and I knew exactly what I was spending it on: taking my true treasures, my children, on a trip we would never forget. I was turning 50, and after all the incredible loss and trauma we had experienced, I decided I was going to take my kids on my dream trip. We flew into Venice for five days of living in a fairy tale, then took the ultimate dream train through the Alps: the Orient Express to Paris. As a mystery writer, I felt it was necessary to take the Orient Express as "research." In Paris we reveled in the city of light and all its magnificent art and my favorite bookshop. We then rented a car and drove to see Josephine Baker's castle. And after that, we spent a few days in my dream wine region: Burgundy.

Selling my jewels paid for our hotel in Venice, our feathered hats for our night on the Orient Express, our hotel in Paris, and so much more.

Now those memories are priceless treasures that can never be cursed or broken.

So, let me encourage you before you start throwing things out the window: sell what you can and do something extraordinary and healing with it.

Chapter 10
Dragonslayer

My favorite mythology scholar, Joseph Campbell, said near the end of every hero's journey, we face a massive dragon guarding life's greatest treasure: the truth of our soul. It's a lesson I learn over and over, but it seems the dragon is bigger this time, with much sharper teeth and claws, and hotter fire-breathing capabilities than ever before.

But guess what? I have experience slaying dragons.

After getting my Masters degree at Harvard, I craved quiet, long walks in the woods, and the company of my favorite humans: children. So I took a one-year teaching position at a Waldorf preschool on an island at the edge of the world — AKA Martha's Vineyard. I knew it would be a good fit when my job interview took place on a blanket under an apple tree, with watermelon and lemonade, and two little kittens romping around me. Martha's Vineyard was a shock for a city girl, coming from fifteen years of living in Hollywood, and one year in Cambridge. All of a sudden I found myself tromping through snow, bringing in my own firewood, having farmer mothers bring in wool from their sheep for the children to card and spin, and grain to grind into flour to bake our bread.

It was like being dropped into a rustic fairy tale.

The island was stunning, and my heart ached with the beauty of the light from the water, the moss-covered forests, twisting trees, and charming houses.

It also ached with my old friend, loneliness, but I was eventually able to create a community for myself by teaching preschool to the children by day and teaching belly dance to the mothers by night, a perfect combo. The first Waldorf celebration I was asked to create on the island happened to be slaying a dragon.

In September, Waldorf preschools celebrate "Michaelmas," a holiday about the battle between St. Michael and a dragon, a metaphor for the battle between dark and light, good and evil. I happen to like dragons, but the mothers explained to me that for this ritual, the dragon represents our innermost fears, our inner negativity, and darkness. It's a time of year when the sunlight grows less and less and humans must go inward, lighting their own inner lights to get through the dark winter.

This I could understand.

I love a metaphor—tell me a good story and I'm all in. Joseph Campbell said, "The metaphor is the mask of God through which eternity is to be experienced." Well said!

My preschoolers and I spent the week before Michaelmas making a dragon's head out of a basket and sheep's wool from Lucy's farm. All the Waldorf families met on a beautiful white powder sand cove on a sunny September afternoon. Some of the children dressed up as knights with pretend swords, and the rest lined up under a long green piece of silk, with me at the head of the dragon. There was storytelling and drumming as we all danced down to the beach, till the tiny knights pretended to slay us. I ran into the ocean I my skirt, throwing the dragon head into the sea, while the children cheered.

It's been 17 years since that day. I wish I could vanquish my current dragon so easily, with a little drumming, dancing, and cheering children.

My current dragon is divorce, and it feels like I am constantly battling the feelings of betrayal and primal fears that go along with it. It feels a lot like a vicious dragon blowing relentless white-hot fire on me, and I don't know how to stop it.

Last week I took many walks on Singing Beach to try to calm myself. The light hitting the rocks formed a lighthouse, and the lighthouse was always my symbol for my Dad.

Wherever I went in the world, I would bring him home lighthouses or lighthouse keepers, because he was always a beacon of wisdom, integrity and light.

It became clear to me that there are only two things I want at the end of this divorce: my children and my soul. I realized that I no longer wanted any part of this divorce fight. There is so much darkness being hurled my way, not just from my ex and his vicious band of lawyers, but from my own self.

Joseph Campbell says that in mythology, dragons represent the human ego, and the ego pins us down and holds us there, forming a cage around us.

Ego is what you believe, what you can do, what you think you love, the aim of your life...

But what if you are capable of much greater things than you currently know?

In this divorce, I want to fight for justice, I want a fair outcome, I want to change an unfair system that values the "moneymaker" over the "soulmaker."

But in this fight, I am losing my own soul.

I can no longer sleep. My brain spins in on itself. I wake up drenched in sweat, fear, and grief. It's a losing battle because the longer it continues, the more the kid's future is set on fire, disappearing in a puff of smoke to the lawyers, and for what? My friend, Jen Tracy, posted something last week that said, "I hope when the time comes to bet on yourself, you double down."

So while walking on the beach, I decided to bet on myself and double down. I have always had a magical life. I had an amazing career as a dancer. I performed with so many of my childhood idols and heroes—Paul McCartney, Placido Domingo, The Go-Go's, the B-52's, Berlin, Crissie Hynde...then I wanted to read more and learn more so I went to UCLA and Harvard. I wanted to live in New Orleans and I did. I wanted to be a mother and I did. There is no reason to doubt myself. I have always figured things out in a magical way.

So I made the decision that my ex could have everything—and I immediately felt at peace-- I just wanted my children and my soul.

It's terrifying—I'm 50 and have only worked as a performer, Mom, and writer, none of which have historically provided a good enough living to support my kids.

But hold on, I forgot to mention my most recent job, a job I've learned on the fly: dragonslayer.

So, divorce aside, what if the biggest dragon is just myself, my own ego?

Here's an example of how rude my ego can get: my car is making some very bad noises. First I get angry at my ex for not making sure that his wife and kids are in a safe car. Then I feel helpless because I don't have the money to fix it. Then I get mad at the mechanic because they can't fit me in until Thursday, and I'm like dude—what if it breaks down? (He shrugged). And then I get mad at myself that I don't have an income that would give us a safe car, and then I get terrified that no one will ever want to hire someone trying to find their first real job at the age of 50. Sigh.

Damn dragons.

I told my son when we turned a corner and it sounded like we were landing a plane, "I hope that whatever is wrong with this car is free because I have no way to pay for it." (And guess what? It *was* free!! Turns out the stupid car was just in 4-wheel drive.) So what if I just let go and trust myself that I will figure things out for me and my children as we go? How exactly do I do that? I can tell myself to trust myself all day long, but I won't believe myself.

Hmmmmm, this requires a warm chocolate chip cookie for optimal pondering.

So, I suppose the question is what to do with the dragon and the unrelenting fire, because if I just lay down and surrender I will surely be burnt to a crisp.

So, do I fight it? Kill the dragon with a sword? Get out my firehose and douse the flames, then tame the damn thing? Make it my pet?

Oh I like that idea. I would shrink it into an adorable emerald green dragon and get it a soft pink fluffy circular bed and some treats to chew on, maybe put a bow behind its ear?

But *how* do I tame it? Wild things don't usually want to be tamed and they bite.

(I love the way the "Mother of Dragons" tamed her dragons in Game of Thrones, and I certainly feel I've been in the middle of the fire for a long time, but I prefer to keep my clothes on at this point in my life.)

Campbell has an answer for conquering the dragons called the "soul's high adventure." He says, "Follow your bliss, and do not be afraid, and doors will open where there were only walls." Sounds easy, right? Follow your bliss? So I can eat an endless stream of warm chocolate chip cookies and doors will open? Because I can't think of anything more blissful right now.

I recently read a book called *Red, Hot, and Holy,* and the author, Sera Beak writes, "The important thing to remember about dragons is that they guard a buried treasure. When a dragon appears, it means gold is right behind it if we have the courage to stand our ground and meet it... But let's be real clear: dragons can't be perfumed away with positive affirmations or cleaned up with simple spiritual techniques. ***Dragons rip open our wounds and make a mess.*** On Purpose. Yes, dragons are a terrifying but necessary sacred set-up because they demand courageous action. They test us with unrelenting fire, to find out if we have metabolized all the profound realizations we've acquired thus far on our soul's journey." That sounds about right. I definitely feel ripped open at my core.

How do I rescue myself from myself? I HAVE NO IDEA!!! HHEEELLPP!!! Okay, what is my bliss besides cookies?

For me, following my bliss means spreading love and light and sparkles and laughter and creating — that's when I feel my best. Certain words conjure up bliss for me: rainbows, unicorns, glitter, children, roaring fires, rosy cheeks, warm mittens, whiskers on kittens... oh wait, I'm turning this into the song "My Favorite Things."

Okay, my bliss... writing, dancing, painting, children, theater, rainbows, unicorns, fairy tales, storytelling, libraries, vintage fashion, tutus, feathers, New Orleans jazz, parades, flowers, creativity, good friends, sunshine and beach walks, and of course, warm chocolate chip cookies.

Campbell says, "The demon you swallow gives you its power and the greater life's pain, the greater life's reply."

I hope so. And I hope this holds true for chocolate chip cookies too, because the cookie you swallow gives you its power and the greater the cookie, the greater the cookie's reply, and the greater my behind. So maybe this is not as profound, but it is true, which is something in this age of lies.

Truth is my favorite. I think it might be speaking my truth that will tame or vanquish my dragons. I'm going to try it and see what happens.

Chapter 11
Take Back Valentine's Day

For the first Valentine's in decades that I no longer had a paramour, I felt silly that it made me feel even sadder, but it did. For more than a decade I had received incredible flowers on Valentine's from my ex. When I grew up, my father used to make us all his Valentine's, bringing us balloons and teddy bears. I loved it. He cherished all six of his children, and even though he always joked he'd rather raise baby werewolves than four teenage daughters, we knew how much he loved us.

I always try to make my children feel extra-cherished on Valentine's—sometimes I write everything I love about them on pink polka dots and tape them to their bedroom doors while they sleep. Sometimes I make a trail of rose petals leading them to a new book or stuffed animal. But even with all of that, it was sad that I no longer had my husband there to jump around, waving his arms all day saying "I'm your valentine forever!" Okay, he never actually did this, but in my mind he did. So, the first Valentine's with a husband who was celebrating his new love for his new girlfriend while I cared for the kids at home, my dear friend Tristan called.

Everyone asks how I met Tristan. It was kismet for sure. I came to Cambridge before I started Harvard to find housing. I wanted spiral stairs, a fireplace, somewhere warm and magical, perfect for studying that also allowed my cat, Pazzo. The emails I sent out ahead of time informed me I would never find that in Cambridge for under a thousand dollars a month.

And then I walked into Tristan's house. He had posted an index card at Harvard housing about renting out a room. I arrived and there was the wooden spiral staircase surrounded by purple walls, leading up to a gorgeous two story house with rich gleaming wood wainscoting up the walls, a round living room, Moroccan décor in the living room, melted candelabras, enormous paintings everywhere, a fireplace, runes scattered on the terrace table, and a sunny yellow room with a bay window where I could watch the snow fall while reading. There were French doors, a clawfoot tub, and Tristan's room had leopard print drapes, purple walls, and a massive white tiger sitting on his velvet bed. White tigers and I go way back. I took the room, it was perfect. Tristan was a dreamboat and became one of my best friends. Positive, hilarious, and living a rich life as an artist finding the beauty and magic in everything. We were kindred spirits. In Boston!

So on Valentine's, Tristan asked if he could come up to my greenhouse and have a glass of pink champagne with me. Tristan is one of those people who somehow knows when to show up. He said, "That seems like the right thing to do, right?" He came up and within a half hour, he had transformed my greenhouse into a beautiful pink accented place — turned up the heat (February in Boston!), turned on soaring classical music, brought out pink napkins, pink champagne, called a few friends, who all came over surprisingly on a random afternoon on the spur of the moment. Then, he brought in a small box on ice, opened it, passed out flat pink envelopes and instructed us all to open them. Inside the small envelopes? Pink lady butterflies. A hundred of them. They happily fluttered out into my greenhouse in the most magical way. Tristan had laid out cotton balls soaked in Gatorade and they drank and flew and landed in our hair, on our hands, on our shoulders.

So when you feel like a total failure at love, it's nice to see how it shows up in the arrival of your best friend with a box of butterflies under his arm, laughter on his lips, and a swirl of magic one afternoon that makes your heart lift a little after a tremendously heavy time.

Chapter 12
Revenge Body 2

This morning I made the best waffles I have ever tasted.

I often make waffles for my kids for breakfast, especially when I have berries and whipped cream on hand. And of course, as the cook, it is my duty to taste them to make sure they are delicious. I am of the opinion that if you add enough butter and warm maple syrup to anything, including cardboard, it will taste delicious, but this morning's waffles, even without butter and syrup, got an A+.

This is a huge achievement for me as cooking is not one of my talents, but with quarantine happening, I have been cooking much more elaborate meals, and some are even edible!

Another benefit of quarantine is that I am exercising a lot more. Before quarantine, I would go to yoga here and there, or dance around my house, but now I take frequent "jogs," meaning I put on my favorite music and plod along like an old Clydesdale, slow and steady, but with a jaunty high step.

When my teens are with me, they beg me to stop. They say my high-stepping slow pace is embarrassing, even though there are no other people around to observe said high-stepping. I now have answers to unanswerable questions like: "If a tree falls in the forest with no one around, does it make a sound?" Yes! "If a parent high-steps around their neighborhood when there's no one around, do their teens feel embarrassed?" Yes.

So, another quarantine activity that I have started is what I call "Mind-wanders. These are the delightful new activities of worrying about things that will most likely NOT happen, but might someday. Someone else might call these "mind-wanders" ANXIETY, like Claire Bidwell Smith, who wrote the book I am currently reading called Anxiety: The Other Phase of Grief. Claire is a renowned grief therapist, and her book caught my eye when she wrote about the physiological panic attacks that can happen with grief. I get these and they are most unpleasant, in fact, one might say they are downright scary when your heart starts pounding and suddenly you can't breathe and you have to pull over your car to take a minute. But I don't call it anxiety because I don't like labels. She says anxiety, I say "Mind-wanders."

As a new divorcee (three months!) in the middle of a pandemic, my latest worry is that my ex-husband will bring one of his new spring chicken paramours to my son's 8th grade graduation.

Now, you might say:

You're worrying about 8th grade graduation? But your son is in 7th grade.

Yes, I know, he will be in 8th grade next year.

But that event is more than a year away.

Yes, I know.

Who even knows what will be happening with graduations a year from now with quarantining and virus mania?

Yes, I know, but I need to start jogging and doing crunches JUST IN CASE my ex decides to bring a paramour to a POSSIBLE graduation next year, or the year after, or whenever!

I know, this sounds crazy, but try telling that to my mind. It won't listen.

And I guess motivation is always a good thing, at least it's getting me off my very cozy couch and out into the world to see the stunning flowers and breathe the fresh air with the added bonus of working my heart, getting my blood flowing, lifting my spirits and maybe even my behind—I see no downside.

Except for the mental spiral that is hard to stop.

It's kind of like when my sisters are coming to visit me and all of a sudden I start doing crunches so my stomach will be flatter than theirs when they arrive. I take a night off from crunching on buttered popcorn and instead crunch my abs, imagining how they will coo, "Your stomach is so flat, you bee-otch! What are you doing?"

I will giggle to myself, shrug and say, "Oh nothing, this is just the way I am! Fast metabolism I guess."

I play out this fantasy in my mind, but the problem is, I start doing crunches the NIGHT BEFORE they arrive, therefore my stomach is NOT FLAT when I pick them up from the airport, but there's usually are, because they actually exercise regularly and don't start the night before.

I can trace this behavior back to my teenage years, when I decided to try out for my high school gymnastic team. I put on some sporty shorts and lunged my way upstairs to the kitchen. My Dad said, "Where are you going?" I said, "The gym. I'm trying out for the gymnastics team." My Mom said, "When are the tryouts?" I mumbled, "Tomorrow," as I lunged out the door to the sound of their laughter.

I went to the recreation center down the street that evening and lifted some barbells, did a few handstands, and stretched my splits. I thought, "I can do splits, backbends, walkovers and even a handspring on occasion without falling on my head. I'll be shocked if I don't make it."

The next morning I went to tryouts. The coaches were surprised to see me there since I was the girl who always brought a forged note from her parents excusing her from PE, for various reasons like mysterious sprains, or internal injuries invisible to the naked eye.

The coaches had me do a somersault on the beam. I fell off. They had me do a leap on the beam. I fell off. They had me do the hardest trick of all—a back walkover on the high beam. I stood there on that high beam in my sporty shorts, one toe pointed in the air, both arms straight up, praying I wouldn't miss and end up in traction for a year. I remembered my old gymnastic teacher's words, "Back walkovers on the beam are easier than front walkovers because when going backwards, your arms are in a straight line from your legs. It's actually really hard to miss the beam in a back walkover." I prayed this was true, and with great bravado given to me by my sporty shorts, which held some kind of mystical power to make me feel athletic, I went for it.

I went for it and I stayed on the freaking beam, cheering for myself when I didn't fall off, well, cheering in my mind because I didn't want to act too cocky. I acted like I did walkovers on high beams a hundred times a day. I dusted off my hands and said, "What next?" They asked to see a round-off-back-handspring, which I had bragged I could do, even though I couldn't. But again, my gymnastic teacher always said it was psychological. You just have to go for it and think "STRONG." Now in hindsight, I have to say he left out a little something, like I would also need to have the skills for the trick, a little something called arm strength and leg strength and flexibility. But I went for it, my arms collapsed, and although I did not end up in traction, I did end up hurting my neck and maybe spraining my ankle.

Now, you have to understand that when I heard my old gymnastic teacher's voice in my head, it echoed like the 1975 TV show, "*Kung Fu.*" If you aren't lucky enough to have been exposed to this show, Wikipedia describes it as an "American action-adventure martial arts western drama," which could be a way to describe my entire high school experience. In the show, blind Master Po relays his wisdom to his young student, whom he calls "Grasshopper."

I don't know why I listened to my gym teacher with his red hair cut in a military buzz, complemented by his red brush moustache, and legs paler than a sheet of paper in his own sporty shorts: white, short, tight. I probably shouldn't have been watching so many Kung Fu episodes, which my Dad loved. He had an endless cache of jokes involving calling us kids "Grasshopper," like "Grasshopper, come eat your dinner." "Grasshopper, put on our pajamas and go to bed." Now that I think about it, I don't know why we laughed so hard when he started his "Grasshopper" jokes. In any case, the words of my gymnastic coach echoed in my mind like the words of Grasshopper's teacher.

But back to the action-adventure drama that was my high school experience. I also tried out for the dance team, the cheerleading team, and even the pep squad and made all of them!!

Just kidding.

I made none of them. I DID make the tennis team where I played in the #10 spot out of ten girls, and most likely, only ten tried out. I DID get into the chess club, even though I didn't know how to play chess, and I do remember feeling like a graceful high-stepping circus pony stumbling into a pride of wild African Chess lions when I walked into that room. These lions looked less like lions and more like skinny nerdy boys who may or may not have ever talked to a girl before.

And to be fair to my horrible high school list of rejections, my goal in trying out for all these teams was not to be on the teams. I just wanted to have my photo in the yearbook more than once. Why? Who knows what I was thinking? I was probably "mind-wandering" and imagining myself in forty years as a sad loner who could sit in the gutter with a bottle of vodka, reassuring herself she wasn't always a lonely hobo, she once was so wonderful that she had not one, but *three* photos in her high school yearbook.

When I got rejected from song leading, I came home in my new sporty shorts my Mom had bought me, and my Mom said, "How did it go?" I burst into tears and she hugged me saying, "Oh Marci, I think you need to start working out for these things earlier than the night before."

She was right.

I finally started listening to my mother, which is why I'm starting my crunches now, during quarantine, just in case I have to meet one of my ex's paramours in the future. This is one of those parts of divorce that you never hear about and can't really understand until you go through it—having to interact with the person who betrayed you, who destroyed your family, who, if there was any justice in the world, you would be seeking a *Count of Monte Cristo* level of revenge on, instead of smiling and laughing and tossing your hair with them as you sit with them and their new love to cheer on your beloved child together.

I can't explain it, but it feels a bit like this: The Creature of the Black Lagoon has ripped your heart out, then has slimed your children over and over again, and you have spent years holding your children in the middle of the night, rebuilding them and your heart. Now some time has passed and post-divorce society demands that you sit down and have tea with the Creature, even though you will be covered in black slime afterwards.

Don't you think you would feel better seeing the creature if you feel "strong" which is code word for "have a stomach so flat and legs so toned you can rock a string bikini in your 50's?"

And then I think, can *anyone* rock a bikini or a speedo in their 50's? I guess at this point, who cares? I'm half a century old! I have two beautiful children! My rocking body has gone the way of the dinosaurs! Time to cultivate my mind and soul, so people will say, what a gorgeous mind that woman has! And a divine soul! Such kindness! And so hilarious! But then I see Shakira and J. Lo. and my pro-fitness sister-in-law, Nicole, and I think, damn it! They are middle-aged Moms that can do the splits on a pole and rock a leotard! (AM I showing my age? Does anyone use the word "leotard" anymore?) I really have no excuse, not pregnancies, not middle age. If they can do it, so can I! I know, I know! They defy science, age, culture, the world! But they inspire me too, and I think if they can do it, I can do it!

All this talk of toned bodies is making me look sadly at the pool of syrup and dash of whipped cream left behind on my waffle plate. I had planned to finish it off by mopping it up with my son's remaining waffles. But I'm SURE J. Lo, Shakira and Nicole would just walk away and go eat a carrot and do some pull-ups on a nearby tree.

But it seems wrong to waste something as valuable as Vermont maple syrup which costs nearly the same as a bar of gold. And the whipped cream *is* organic, which is code for "healthy."

But I swear on my life, it will be a sad day when I choose to eat carrots over waffles with strawberries and whipped cream.

Because as Mae West so eloquently said, "The only carrots I care about are the carats in a diamond."

Amen, Mae.

But even better than diamonds?

Whipped cream and strawberries on a hot buttered waffle smothered in warm maple syrup.

Chapter 13
Transform His Half of the Closet!

After my husband left that horrible morning, I threw all of his clothing into garbage bags, intending to take them all outside for a bonfire. But the bags were so heavy I couldn't lift them. I called movers to come get everything in the house and put it in storage. We had His and Hers walk-in closets in our master bedroom, and he had redone his floor in gorgeous gleaming dark wood. I wanted to rip the ugly white carpet out of my closet too, but he said we didn't have enough money to do both, so we would just do his. After all his things were gone, the closet was incredibly depressing, like the Grinch had just visited and taken everything. My bestie bought me some sage and we smudged it, meaning the Native American practice of lighting sage on fire and waving the smoke around a space while saying, "I clear out all negative and toxic energy and welcome in only positive and loving energy." After smudging, I went to Home Depot, bought some buckets of bubble gum pink paint and paintbrushes, came home and started painting the closet formerly known as His. My 80-year-old mother insisted on helping me, and we took turns transforming that depressing closet into a gorgeous happy luscious shrine to my favorite color. In the end, it was a bigger job than it seemed, and I hired someone to finish it.

People who saw it said, "I guess you're never planning on selling this house." It is a pet peeve of mine when people paint their walls or design something in their house for some future owner they've never met. It's my house right now, I'm living in it, the next owners can paint it whatever color they like, but while I'm here, I want it to make my heart sing. And pink always makes my heart sing.

That closet turned out to be gorgeous—it literally glowed with a rosy hue, and I filled it with my costumes, wild wigs, sparkling handbags, witty jaunty hats, feathers, ballgowns, and all sorts of beautiful things. It worked! His energy was eradicated from that closet and now, a dark dreary hole in the wall is transformed into sparkles and joy and beauty.

I moved my transformation out into the rest of the house, replacing all photos of him with photos of the kids running and laughing; moving my antique vanity that I loved and my ex hated. into my bedroom. And my purple desk. I saged my bed over and over, but found that the "married" energy wasn't leaving, so I finally invested in a new mattress. With each thing that disappeared from our life together, I felt lighter, more free, and closer to moving onwards and upwards.

Chapter 14
Finding My Own Invincible Summer

This morning I woke up to rain and went outside to drag in my patio cushions, and the air smelled salty, like the sea. I thought, "I really don't want to be spending my time doing this. I want to be writing, baking, exercising, packing for our upcoming move..." But the sea air softly landed on my cheeks, and I smiled as I had a fleeting childhood memory of being with my grandparents in San Diego, with their avocado tree and our walks to the beach. It made me feel a moment of warm joy, when you don't have a specific memory, but just the feeling is there. I heard the birds calling to each other in the treetops, the raindrops soft and cool on my skin, the smell of wet earth and pine trees, the bright pop of pink from my flowers, and I felt a moment of beauty, my own "invincible summer" pushing back against a world flinging too many tears around right now. I found this little piece of writing by Albert Camus the other day that really resonated with me:

"In the midst of hate, I found there was, within me, an invincible love. In the midst of tears, I found there was, within me, an invincible smile. In the midst of chaos, I found there was, within me, an invincible calm. I realized, through it all, that in the midst of winter, I found there was, within me, an invincible summer. And that makes me happy. For it says that no matter how hard the world pushes against me, within me, there's something stronger, something better, pushing right back."

There is a lot of hoopla on the internet about whether Camus wrote this entire quote, or just the part about his "invincible summer" as found in his essay, "Return to Tipassa."

Whether Camus wrote it or some other great writer, or even Owen the Mad Walker of Orem, is irrelevant to its resonance in my heart, but I'd love to find out if anyone out there knows! In any case, who is Owen, the Mad Walker of Orem? When I was a child growing up in Orem, among the orchards full of apples, cherries, pears, and the meadows of mountain wildflowers that have now been turned into Target parking lots, nearly every day we would see a man walking all over town, with his long white beard, so long it passed all the pockets on his overalls. My parents would always say, "There's Owen!" And I would watch him out my car window as we passed by, just walking, carrying nothing. We saw him at all hours, morning, noon and night, all over town, seemingly spending his days just endlessly walking. No one ever said anything more than, "There's Owen." I have no idea who he was, but here I am, forty five years later, remembering Owen and his overalls and white beard.

I guess this memory of Owen is mine to create whatever I want. Should I make him a happy hobo, wandering and exploring the town all day, pulling crisp apples off the tree when he's hungry, watching the ladybugs and butterflies softly flutter by, or hearing his boots crunch in the snow? Did he smell the wood smoke from our fireplaces and look at the homes lit from within and wish he had his own family? Had he suffered some great tragedy that had left its mark so deep in his soul he could no longer chop wood, read a book, or drive a truck? Or had he decided he didn't want to be part of the hamster wheel of life, working-working-working to amass more-more-more, when all Owen needed was a pair of overalls and a comb for his beard? Or maybe he had worked his job, made a gazillion dollars, raised his family, and was now free to do whatever he wanted? And he wanted to walk.

As the years pass for me, and I endure my own share of tragedies, losing the people I love so much, I think, maybe Owen was onto something. Maybe his way of "pushing back" against a world with way too much hate, chaos, and tears, was to keep things simple: take a walk.

I just put the ladder away in my shed, the ladder I had dragged out to climb to get my cat out of a tree. I leaned it against the wet wood of the shed, and was hit in the face with a spray of water from the flowers draped over the shed. I came back inside, dried my face, made my cappuccino and sat down to write about Camus, but ended up writing about Owen. My children are sleeping upstairs in their beds. My coffee is warm in my hand. The dogs are sprawled on the floor, keeping my bare feet warm, all three cats are sitting like works of art, looking out the window. And I think, this is my own "invincible summer." If this moment is the best I ever get for the rest of my life, it will be enough.

Chapter 15
Why Don't Lawyers Take Fairy Dust as Payment?

I woke up this morning thinking of Kim, my soul sister. I remember when I met her, it felt like I was recognizing a part of myself. We met as fairies of course, in a West Hollywood Globe production of *Midsummer Night's Dream*. I remember reading something by Anais Nin, where she talked about recognizing a soul mate, how it felt like you were once one whole, and your whole was split in two, and when you find that other half, and you recognize each other, it's painful to be apart. All is right with the world when you are together, even better when you are intertwined.

I woke up remembering how Kim always wanted to make my dreams come true. For example, she knew that ever since I was 5-years-old, for every single birthday candle wish, and every first star wish, I had wished for the same thing—a horse. I was one of those horse crazy girls. I read every book I could find on horses, and studied the proper way to mount and dismount. My parents didn't have money for a horse, so I had a stable of imaginary horses that I had named and would ride around in the fields and meadows next to my house. So for one birthday, Kim gave me giant horse slippers that neighed when you pressed their ears.

For another birthday, I was at my parent's house, feeling sad and cold because my Dad refused to turn the heat up for me. I was sitting on the couch in my giant faux fur coat when the doorbell rang. It was a package for me from Kim. I eagerly opened it up and inside was a beautiful tutu with rainbow ribbons and a matching wand. My heart sang when I put it on and started dancing around my house, my parents laughing and shaking their heads as I twirled through the kitchen where they were cooking dinner.

I remember one birthday when Kim put a tiara on my head and had me sit on my big pink bed because she had a surprise.

She ran into the back of our house and I could hear whispers and giggles as she prepared the surprise which turned out to be... a parade!

Kim knew I loved parades, and so she created one for my birthday. She had a bunch of our friends gather in the back room of our house, then she turned on my favorite parade music which was the "Topsy Turvy" song from Disney's *Hunchback of Notre Dame*. I used to play it for the AIDS children I worked with. I would bring maracas and ribbons sticks and we would have a parade around the residential shelter where they lived. I would carry the kids who couldn't walk, or they would cheerfully wave their sticks and move along on their crutches or in their wheelchairs. The kids loved parades as much as I did.

Kim dipped into my magic bag and gave all my friends my ribbon sticks, magic wands, glitter and rose petals to throw on me, leis to put around my neck and they all looped through our kitchen and back in front of me again—most laughing awkwardly, feeling silly, but Kim was exuberant, and I was thrilled. At the end she put a crown on my boyfriend's head of dark curls and presented me with him as a gift.

It was wonderful.

Back in December, my sister, Maria, was visiting me. I received a ping from my lawyer. She took my phone and read the email, then she texted our little sister.

"Her lawyer just quit."

"What? Why?"

"Because she offered to pay him in fairy dust."

"Sigh."

Now, you may be wondering what the heck?

And before you throw me under a rainbow unicorn bus on the way to fairyland, let me explain.

Maria's plane was delayed by hours, so we were binge-watching *Stranger Things*, sitting on my Lovesac couch, the one I can't get off of without some major rolling and somersaulting-- thank goodness for my years in the circus. My lawyer had been threatening to quit my case for some time because I owed him money, but after another failed attempt to settle the case, he actually did it.

So rude!

But it turned out to be good.

I really liked my lawyer. He was cute, with a deep soothing voice and a great storyteller. He also was a really good person, highly ethical and super smart. However, this whole process was so deeply emotional, and I often felt like molten lava inside, and not the good molten lava you find in the middle of a chocolate cake, but the fiery kind you find in an ugly gray mountain. So I would see his mouth moving, but I couldn't hear him talking. I didn't want to discuss anything with him-- I just wanted him to make it all go away with the best deal possible. I had already given him boatloads of money, but with my bank accounts frozen, I was way behind on paying him.

Also, in his email to me explaining his actions, he actually cited the fact that I offered to pay him in fairy dust as a reason for his quitting, elaborating by saying I didn't "respect the process." What? Me? How strange that I wouldn't respect the process of my family falling apart in such a vicious and painful way. How strange that I didn't respect a process that hurt my children more than they had already been hurt, and therefore me.

But he was right. I hated the process. And fairy dust would have helped a lot.

After he quit, I didn't feel bad—I felt liberated and free of the crushing waste of money.

Anything spent on lawyers was taking away from the kid's futures.

So, when January rolled around and we had a court date set for something that wouldn't have moved us any closer to resolution, I told my ex, I'm showing up by myself. Annihilate me further, crush me further, I no longer care, because and I will no longer throw money out the window. You can show up with your team of lawyers, in addition to your father who is a lawyer, and yourself, who is a lawyer, and you are all going against me by myself. Does that seem like a good use of resources? This whole process has dragged on long enough."

Usually when I called him he'd scream some epithet in my ear and hang up, but I caught him in a sane moment and said, "Let's just sneak to the conciliator. Don't tell your lawyers. We won't leave until the agreement is signed. At this point, I don't want anything, just the kids."

He agreed and we did it the next day. Of course his lawyers found out and tried to intervene, but he shut them down and we showed up and we both just came to an agreement in an hour.

Now don't get me wrong. I'm terrified of our future and how I will support my kids. But I said to myself, "What are you afraid of?"

A friend of mine posted this: "I hope when the time comes to bet on yourself, you double down."

And I thought, what the heck, Marci? You have always had an extraordinary life. ALWAYS. What are you afraid of? Well, for starters, I'm 50 and have been a stay at home mom. My previous career was belly dancer and circus acrobat, two things I can't do anymore unless people are impressed with my skills rolling off my couch. That I can still do.

But you can write. You can think. You can create. TRUST YOURSELF! BET ON YOURSELF!

DOUBLE DOWN!

So just like that, like the flip of a switch, or the flip of a circus acrobat, I believed in myself again. It wasn't gradual. Or maybe it was and I just didn't notice. It was one minute from "I'm terrified my life is over" to "I'll be fine."

How about that?

So in the end, I'm glad my lawyer quit. If he hadn't, if he had been able to take fairy dust over money, the divorce process would have continued to crush my soul, and take it's toll on me and the kids.

And now... we're free.

And we can rebuild.

And do you know what helps rebuild broken hearts? Fairy dust. I'm pouring some over my head right now.

And one more thing—when I send my lawyer his final check, I will be including some pink glitter in the envelope.

Chapter 16
Conciliation, Jubilation, and Periwinkles

I was walking my dog, Snickerdoodle, on the beach when my lawyer called me and advised Conciliation. He said Conciliation is better than Mediation, which didn't work for us at all, because you meet with an objective lawyer who reviews your case and tries to give you an impartial view, advising you on what the outcome would likely be if it went to trial. It's supposed to save you from wasting money on a trial. As he talked, I tried to listen, but I was distracted by Snickerdoodle bouncing along the beach like a flying reindeer, leaping over sea puddles with all four paws in the air. I call him Jubi at the beach because he is so jubilant, running as fast as he can, occasionally looking over his shoulder to make sure I'm near. He bounds to greet other dogs, then turns around and races back to me, his ears flying in the wind. He gallops around me as fast as he can and races back towards the other dogs. His joy is contagious, and he makes everyone at the beach laugh with his antics.

When my lawyer heard my reluctance, he said I would love the guy doing it, that he was a "teddy bear." Good analogy, now I was intrigued. Who *wouldn't* love to meet a life-sized law-practicing teddy bear? If lawyers looked like teal teddy bears, wouldn't court be so much nicer? I agreed and spent an inordinate amount of time thinking about what the "conciliator" would look like. Would he have round ears? Kind eyes? A furry pot belly?

Coincidentally, I call Snickerdoodle the "Teddy Bear Scoundrel" because he looks like an oatmeal teddy bear with his unruly hair falling over his big brown eyes, and he's a scoundrel for sure. There isn't a slipper around the Snicker hasn't tried to eat. Sometimes I imagine his photo on a WANTED poster in the Old West: WANTED! The Teddy Bear Scoundrel! For crimes of tearing apart slippers and jumping on the counter to eat the kid's spaghetti!

And by the way, Snickerdoodle has a lot of different names. When we got him, we let my ex name him because my ex didn't like pets, and we were hoping it would help him bond with him. My ex named him Dizzy, as in Dizzy Gillespie, because all our other pets are named after musicians: Ella, Monk, Bootsy, and now Dizzy. Dizzy is a good name for him, because he's a little crazy, but I always felt like he should be named after a cookie.

After my ex left, I renamed Ella to call her something more suited to her personality: Miss Pepper Caliente or El Diablo. I renamed Monk, our old cat, Whipped Cream Marshmallow Fluffy Tummy, for obvious reasons, and Bootsy got to keep her name because she looks like she's wearing little white boots.

And I renamed Dizzy-- Snickerdoodle.

But the pets refuse to answer to their new names, so now I have to throw their original names into their new names and it gets complicated.

You can probably see how my thinking can complicate things. My ex is trying to get a divorce, I'm trying to stay in my rainbow marshmallow world and pretend this isn't happening. You see the problem?

When I showed up at Conciliation (in my tutu and my sparkles shoes), the Conciliator looked like a regular human, with regular human ears and no fur. However, he did have kind eyes and a comforting voice, so I suppose I get the teddy bear connection. And as he spoke, trying to talk me into an agreement, I imagined him prancing along the beach on four paws. It made the whole process less painful.

After reviewing the facts, the teddy bear offered up his opinion.

I said no way am I agreeing to this madness.

Instead of shaking his head and staring at the ceiling like others do when frustrated with me, he said, "What part of this makes you feel bad?"

Oh Teddy Bear… what part of this makes me feel bad?

ALL OF IT!!!!!

1. I hate divorce. I didn't ask for this, and I did nothing to deserve this, except fall in love with the wrong person.

2. I hate that my children are suffering. I hate that my son got in the car a while back and rocked back and forth, sobbing, "This isn't real! This isn't real! This isn't real!"

3. I hate feeling betrayed and hurt.

4. I hate talking about money. (I'm not a money person, and in fact, I don't understand the point of exchanging dirty green money. Why is it green? Who put all those ugly symbols on it? Why isn't it pink or covered in rainbows? Who decided it had value? Who decided that a green piece of paper with a 20 on it was more valuable than a green piece of paper with a 5 on it, and why must I go along with this fantasy? If I had my way, I would want everyone to pay me in fairy dust, aka glitter. It's much prettier than green paper. I also would prefer to pay people in glitter. But alas, no one will take my fairy dust as payment, at least no one over the age of 10, so I am stuck dealing in green paper.)

Dear Teddy Bear Conciliator, ALL OF THIS MAKES ME FEEL BAD!!

I told a shaman that I get confused whenever anyone talks about the divorce because there's so much emotion swirling in my head. She told me I needed to have a mantra and asked me to clearly state what I wanted.

I said, "I want this over with a fair and just settlement."

So she said, "Say those words to yourself over and over whenever you have to talk about the divorce."

I didn't believe something so simple would work, but it did! It helped to clear my mind every time I was in a meeting with lawyers and accountants and they started boring me to tears with talk of taxes and capital gains.

Yuck.

Can we get back to unicorns and rainbows bouncing on pink marshmallows?

Sigh.

ANYWAY, after hours and hours of Conciliation, the Teddy Bear talked me into accepting a deal. I'm not even sure what the deal was. By the end, my head was spinning and I couldn't hear a word or understand what anyone was saying. I just wanted to go home and bury my tear-stained face in Snickerdoodle's fur.

I drove home and I didn't feel good about any of it.

It's all sooooooo sad!!!! Can I just say that again?

It's so sad!!! It's sad that love doesn't always last forever.

It's sad that we lost our family, the family I thought I'd have forever, the four of us.

It's sad that he quit loving me.

It's sad that I lost the man I thought was my soul mate and true love.

It's sad that I wasn't able to make him feel loved, adored, and cherished.

It's sad that the kids have cried themselves to sleep umpteen times.

It's sad that I hold them and kiss their tears away and there's not a darn thing I can do to fix this.

It's sad that they won't get to have an intact family as they grow.

You know what else this is?

SCARY!!

SCARY AS HELL!!

I'm scared of how this will inform my kid's future relationships, and I'm not even sure I want them to go through relationships, because I am terrified of them getting their hearts broken like mine.

I'm scared of them building their life with someone and having it torn away.

I'm scared of their sleepless nights, their burning bones...

I'm scared they have learned the fairy tale isn't real.

I know the ax comes for everyone, every single one of us, and that's the great promise of life—you will have your heart broken over and over.

But I guess the other promise is that you will feel your heart soar. You will fall in love, you will hang on their every word, it will feel like starlight is dancing around the two of you when you look at each other, it will feel like it's the two of you against the world, and you will know intimate things about each other that no one else knows. You will know you have each other's back, and you will picture growing old with them, the ugly scratchy dirt brown cardigan he will wear, how he will shuffle when his hair turns gray, and you will love him even more in his vulnerability.

But now they have learned it can all be taken away.

You can love someone and he will give you a diamond ring with three diamonds on it, saying it represents his love for you and your children, and that he considers it his great honor to hold those three hearts in his hands, and then he will crush them all.

WTF!!!

It's sad!

But... those hearts will mend, hopefully stronger than before. In Japan, they mend broken bowls with gold, making them more beautiful than they were before.

Maybe that's us, mended with gold.

And maybe the fairy tale is that you will see incredible things in life, taste amazing things, hear music so transcendent you will feel you are touching the face of light, witness miracles every day that will take your breath away—the diamonds falling out of the sky when the sun shines a certain way on falling snow; autumn leaves the swirling like golden confetti; a forest of pink blossoms; the warm brown eyes and jubilant prance of the Teddy Bear Scoundrel.

After Conciliation, I felt like I'd come from the boxing ring, so I took the kids and Snickerdoodle to sit on the rocks at the beach, and told them how the enormous rocks worn smooth by the crashing waves are grounding to me and make me feel solid. We sat on the rocks, not talking, just watching the sun dance on the ocean while Snickerdoodle raced up and down the sand, making us, well, snicker.

I looked down at the rocks and saw a periwinkle shell, which is a tiny gorgeous purple spiral that attaches itself to rocks. If you pick it up and hold it gently in your hand and softly hum or sing, the periwinkle slug actually comes dancing out of its shell. I'm not making this up.

No one ever believes me when I tell them about Periwinkles, so I take them to the rocks and show them. After my brother's brutal divorce, I took him and my sisters out on the rocks in the sea. Within a few minutes, every one of them was holding a periwinkle and humming gently, cooing in disbelief and laughing like children when the creatures came dancing out of their shells.

The kids know all about the magic of Periwinkles, and whenever we are on the rocks at the beach, you will see all three of us holding the purple spirals in our cupped hands and humming softly.

And I think that is what I want for them. I want to cup their battered hearts and gently hum until they dance.

Maybe that's the real fairy tale: a gentle touch and a soft song can make a sea slug dance right out of its spiral shell.

If that's not a miracle I don't know what is.

And then Snickerdoodle bounded over, splashing the Periwinkles back into the sea, and we followed his jubilant prance, mimicking him, arm in arm, back to the car.

Chapter 17
I Looked for Joy and the Sneaky Trickster Was in the Shoe Department at Bergdorfs!

Now I've never been one to wear a boring shoe. I like them pink and I like them sparkly. However, I have all sorts of fun things like super high arches and pinky toes that hurt due to breaking in tiny ice skates, so pretty much the only shoes I can wear are terribly ugly-- Uggs or Birkenstocks.

Now don't get me wrong, I still wear beautiful shoes, even if it's only while lying in my bed, in which case they are called my "reclining shoes" or to add sparkle and beauty into my closet, in which case they are called "Closet Candy." So after he left, I treated myself to my first pair of designer shoes. While he was gallivanting around with his girlfriends, I took the kids and my Mom to NYC for a theater trip. We stayed at The Plaza, a hotel that heals all my troubles immediately. We went to see "Kinky Boots" and "Hello Dolly" with Bette Midler, both of which rocked our world. The final morning of our trip, I popped out while everyone was asleep to get Starbucks. I was passing Bergdorfs, and normally I don't like department stores—too big and blah for me, but sometimes I like to walk through a beautiful shoe department because it's like going to a bakery and ordering everything, but no calories! I never buy anything, I just admire the creativity and beauty. But this time, well, I didn't know there was a big shoe sale going on. I popped in for a quick look, and lo and behold, came upon an insane pair of glitter reptile Louboutin ankle boots in just my size for 70% off. What? I don't wear reptile patterns and I don't wear ankle boots, but these were gorgeous, and on sale, so I got them. Then a gorgeous pair of luscious cranberry velvet YSL heels, and though I had hip surgery and I can't really wear heels, I decided some things are worth the sacrifice—these were beautiful. As I walked out, I spied a pair of Gucci sneakers with the word "LOVED" in rainbow crystals across the top. And I thought, you know what? I think I deserve a pair of sneakers that remind me I am loved. I don't feel loved—I feel heartbroken and humiliated, so if nothing else, at least my shoes love me. So I got them too. It was the best shoe shopping spree ever in my life. I still feel warm and gooey inside when I think about it.

Oh and I also bought a pair of pink glitter UGGS that I wear nearly every day and I love them as I'm walking on sparkles.

So it wasn't just shoes. My entire wardrobe became more colorful and sparkly after he left. It felt like the more pain I was in, the more colorful my wardrobe became. Like Frida Kahlo, who always said that her wardrobe grew in color as her body grew in pain from her car accident.

I don't know why, but it seemed like I needed to sparkle head to toe, wear tutus and colorful dresses, every single day. If I ever dressed normal, I felt sad. So I dressed to cheer myself, and it did help. Dressing pretty makes me feel swishy, makes me move differently through the world, with more sass. And it never stopped—nearly two years later and I still have the most colorful and sparkly wardrobe around. It makes me feel happy, warm, and joyful—and honestly, anything that makes me feel that way at this point, I'll take it.

Chapter 18
Badass Bonfire MixTape

Burn Baby Burn!

Darling Divas,

Sometimes you just have to make a bonfire and burn up divorce memories. When I was moving recently, I came across my attorney's file of all my divorce documents and felt that old nausea start to rise. I went out to my fire pit, started a fire, and as I watched the flames burn higher and higher, I felt good. The only thing missing? Music that would dissolve my rational mind and touch me deep in my soul. So I sat next to my fire, my face flushed from the warmth of the flames, and made my Badass Bonfire Mix full of songs that made me laugh, made me cry, made me mad, made me feel empowered and free, and best of all, made me dance. It was a glorious experience. My kids peeked out at me from their bedroom windows, then went back to their teenage world, leaving me to dance and sing out my grief.

These songs are the tip of the iceberg as I'm constantly remembering and discovering new kick ass songs. Here are some of my favorites as inspiration for you to find your own.

> Pick Yourself Up — All Versions from Fred Astaire to Nat King Cole (This is my number one favorite song — just try listening to it and not dancing!)
> I Am Here — Pink
> Shut Up and Let Me Go — Ting Tings
> These Boots Are Made for Walkin' — Nancy Sinatra

Roar — Katy Perry
I Will Survive — Gloria Gaynor
Survivor — Destiny's Child
Gaslighter — The Chicks
Send my Love to Your New Lover — Adele
Praying — Kesha
Take A Bow — Rihanna
Irreplaceable — Beyonce
You Oughta Know — Alanis Morissette
So What — Pink
F*** You — Lily Allen
Shout Out to My Ex — Little Mix
Piece of My Heart — Janis Joplin
Mama's Broken Heart — Miranda Lambert
Truth Hurts — Lizzo
Soulmate — Lizzo
Hit 'Em Up style-Blu Cantrell
I Get Knocked Down — Chumbawamba
Me Too — Meghan Trainor
Mom — Meghan Trainor
Titanium — David Guetta
The Winner Takes It All — ABBA
Break My Stride — Matthew Wilder
Get Ur Freak On — Missy Elliott
Washing of the Waters — Peter Gabriel
Book of Love — Peter Gabriel
I'm Just a Gigolo (Any version — must sing along at the top of your lungs!)
I Like How It Feels — Enrique Iglesias

Chapter 19
Reclaiming My Loves and My Trip to the Opera

I have always loved opera. When I was 16, my school went to see Turandot at the Capitol Theatre in Salt Lake City. I had never been in the theatre. My parents loved theatre, but it was never in our budget to go. I remember going to see one play together as a family and how hard my Dad laughed. I walked into that ornate beautiful vintage theatre and was swept away into the gorgeous spectacular drama that is opera. I was brought to tears with the singing, and back then, before the internet, I went to my local library, checked out record albums of opera recordings, brought them home to play on my record player. I even pulled out a tape recorder and set it against my record player speakers so I could record a tape of the music to play in my car.

A few years later, I saw Pagliacci was coming to LA with Placido Domingo singing the part of the clown. I was elated. Now I would have to figure out a way to go see it, since I never had any money. I came across an audition in Dramalogue to be a supernumerary in my favorite opera, Pagliacci, at the Dorothy Chandler Pavilion in LA. Supernumeraries are the people you see on an opera stage that don't sing. Franco Zefferelli chose me to ride a vespa onstage during a village scene, wearing a leopard mini skirt. I was thrilled. Now I would be able to hear my favorite aria sung over and over by the world's greatest opera singer, and get paid to do it.

Pagliacci turned out to be an amazing experience. The aria rocked my world every night, and I adored watching the maestro conduct the orchestra, his waving arms like a beautiful dance. I also adored the 45 curtain calls and thousands of roses the singers received each night. I became friends with Placido, who was funny and lovely with my parents, giving them 14th row center seats and meeting them in person. My Dad was so excited to meet him. We sat in the restaurant next door to the theatre waiting for Placido, and my Dad said, "When I shake his hand, I'm going to say God has given you a gift, and you are using that gift, sharing it with the world, and if you lay one hand on my daughter I'm going to kick your ass all the way back to Italy." Placido is actually from Mexico, but I didn't want to spoil my Dad's joke so I just laughed. My Dad was adorable, and protective of me, but I was always able to take care of myself with men. Placido knew my love of theatre and got me free amazing tickets to every opera for the next few years in LA and NYC. I would go to NYC and sometimes see two operas a day by myself — that was often 8 hours a day of opera!! Norma, *La Traviata*, Carmen. Placido sang in some, conducted others, and I happily watched them all, cheering at their curtain calls, soaking in their beauty.

My ex didn't like opera. It was one of the things I let go of while we were together. But when I was planning my dream trip, I remembered it. I dusted off forgotten albums, meaning I pulled them up on my Sonos, and played their soaring voices on my patio while I gardened. I found a place in Venice called Musica Palazzo, where they alternated operas each night. I decided it was the perfect introduction to the opera for the kids, and the scenes moved from room to room, so they wouldn't have to just sit and watch for hours. It was perfect. I really wanted to go see *La Traviata*, but when I thought of how much tragedy we had endured, I decided to go for *Barber of Seville* — it's shorter, and a comedy. We all need to laugh.

We dressed up, clicking across the cobblestone streets in Venice in our high heels, with and Henry in his bow tie. We ate in a magical garden, with twinkle lights and statues, Vino Vino. We crossed magical bridges and ended up down a dark alley, which didn't seem right, but as we turned the corner, there it was: a crumbling palazzo built in the 15th century, lit by candles. The opera was fabulous, and from the first few notes, my heart sang.

So welcome back to the world Marci!! Now you can frolic in the world you love!!

Chapter 20
Charming is Disarming

I'm so deeply and irreversibly hurt by everything that happened, it's easy to slip into the hot itchy robe of hostility, hatred, burning anger, desire for vengeance, justice, revenge. But like I said, that robe doesn't feel good. It just feels easy. When he called at any time, I would answer the phone with a caveman grunt, filled with anger, so there would be no mistaking that I would never ever forgive him. I would hate him forever. There was no hell hot enough for him to burn in forever to make up for the pain he caused my beautiful children, and me. I refused to address emails to him with "Dear" and couldn't even bear to say or write his name, instead calling him Voldemort or "The Douche." After time passed, I realized my nature is not hostile and angry. My nature is kind and cheerful and full of light. And one day, out of the blue, I answered the phone as myself, "Hi!" I said brightly, even knowing it was The Dark One. He was taken aback, caught off guard, "disarmed by my charm." It made me feel good, like myself, to be cheerful, even to a dark harmful person, even to someone undeserving of my charm. I realized that by acting like myself, cheery and kind, I felt better inside. It feels better to be free and light than to be bogged down in a cloak of hatred. And I realized that if I let him turn me into a "Bitter Betty," let him turn me into an angry hostile person, HE HAD WON. No only had he stomped all over me and my children, but he had truly won my soul, and yanked me over to the dark side.

I VOWED I WOULD NOT LET THIS HAPPEN.

And guess what? It felt like I had WON! I rid myself of a marriage built on lies, a marriage to a dark narcissistic sociopath, and I was now free to live my life as I truly am—full of light. I WON! I had emerged from the darkness and anger as my sparkling, bubbly self, with impenetrable boundaries.

I'm free to live my life in unshakeable integrity and honesty—exactly how I like.

And by not succumbing to his mind-numbing intense onslaughts, by NOT becoming a "Bitter Betty," I had become a "Beautiful Badass Babe."

I would not allow my children to watch their mother crumble into bitterness. I would not allow them to see me transform into something hard and brittle. Oh hell no. I would hold my head high, laugh, love, stay soft and open-hearted, with that iron boundary. I would disarm my enemy with charm.

And it worked in a kind of miraculous way.

He was puzzled by my soaring kindness, my open heart.

And weirdly enough, the exact opposite happened—my revenge was exacted because now I was a cheery luminescent person, and he lived in darkness. This made him curious.

Believe me, it wasn't always easy. Both of us would get triggered and lash out at each other. It would take me days to recover. I would block him for ten days so I didn't have to talk to him, to give myself some modicum of control. While I was writing this paragraph, he called to try to change the time for dinner with our son, again. I was agreeable, but the next thing that happened was I got triggered, he got triggered, and we ended up furious with each other and it was awful. I was laughing to myself the entire time that here I am writing a paragraph on being charming and I was being very un-charming. But I'm not perfect. I will fail at being charming. But I'm trying, because it works better for me, for the kids, for everyone.

He can be evil. I will be charming.

Sigh.

It's not easy, but it will get easier over time. That's what I'm told. Ask me in a year and I'll tell you if it's true.

Chapter 21
Rituals for Grieving, Healing, and Transformation

Legend of the Banshees: In ancient Ireland, there are tales of Banshees — ghost-like women who wailed outside people's homes to signal death. The people who viewed them described them in different ways: some said they were beautiful young women, some said they were scary old women, some said they were fairy queens. Those descriptions aren't even close! Make up your mind storytellers! But despite these differences, the details of the stories that stay the same is that the Banshees were grieving women, possibly a supernatural version of the "keening women" in Ireland, professional mourners whose job it was to moan, wail, and lament the dead.

Professional mourners have been a part of the grieving process throughout the history of humans, from ancient Egypt to ancient Mexico to the Bible.

I recently heard a story that when someone dies in China, they hire professional mourners to come to the memorial for the deceased. They CRAWL across the cemetery to the place of the memorial, wailing the name of the deceased and sobbing things like, "Dad! Why oh why did you leave us? How will we survive without you?"

The professional mourners don't know the deceased, but they pretend they do. They get to wail and sob all the things the loved ones are thinking and feeling, but not saying. Why don't we do this at our funerals? I feel like it would be healthy.

And what if we had funerals for our marriages? Instead of divorce court, we could all show up at a special marriage cemetery: Here lies the marriage of Marci and her ex, 1999-2020.

At my my father's funeral I wore a retro navy-blue dress with white anchors on the pockets to honor my father's military service and I spoke in a clear voice that was quite surprising considering how I was shaking on the inside. At Kim's funeral I wore fairy wings, a tutu, and cowgirl boots, and climbed a ladder to sit in a treehouse, which was lit with twinkle lights. I chose not to speak, but I danced instead. As Nikos Kazantzakis said in *Zorba the Greek*, when words no longer suffice, leap up and dance. I think Kim would have loved it up in that treehouse with me.

So when I imagine people CRAWLING through a cemetery (I don't know why I love this visual so much) wailing and sobbing, I imagine them with dirt on their faces, torn clothing, twigs in their hair, and a regular person might think, "That is so morbid and weird!" But I am in an altered state, the state of grieving, so I think, "HOW COOL!" And people get paid to do this?

This might be a good job for me right now.

I read more about the professional mourners in China, learning that after they deliver the eulogy in a sobbing way, backed up by musicians playing sad dramatic music, the music changes to an upbeat tune and a BELLY DANCER takes to the stage to signal that the wailing is done. **In China? A belly dancer? Really? Count me in!**

Once again, I'm totally overqualified for this job — a deeply grieving professional belly dancer! But I'm also perfect for it!

My imagination was captured when I learned about these professional mourners, and I started fantasizing about creating a fashion line of mourning clothes. I'm on the Fashion Council at the Boston MFA and sometimes they pull things from their archives to show us. The thing I remember most was Mary Todd Lincoln's black mourning jewelry. She wore it when she lost her son.

It seems appropriate to have clothing and jewelry that sets apart grieving people from the regular crowds. But my ideas for mourning clothing are different than the somber black ensembles of Victorian times. My grieving fashion line would be pink tutu fairy-style clothing, and it would be torn and shredded and covered in pretend dirt. Part of the look includes dirt on the face and hair ratted to it's largest and wildest, ala Pat Benatar in her music video for "Love is A Battlefield." (Something tell me I watched too much MTV as a teen, since her hair is burned into my brain. But then again, for me, love truly is a battlefield, maybe the most brutal and bloody battlefield of all, so maybe Pat Benatar was some kind of sage.)

I told my bestie, Tristan, of my idea for a new fashion line. Without missing a beat, he said, "Darling, this is called a "meltdown." You've crossed into Crazy Land. Come back! Next you'll want to smear your face with strawberry jam and accent the color with a lollipop and call it fashion. It's just tragic, that's what it is." We laughed really hard imagining me with mud and jam smeared on my face, my hair ratted out, my pink fairy tutu shredded, swaggering about and calling it fashion. It's a vision that isn't that far from how I feel — torn, shredded, covered in dirt.

But he had a point.

After the tremendous loss in my life over the past two years, three people that I loved so Deeply madly truly — my beloved father, soul mate, and marriage — I am deep in grief.

Sometimes it feels like I'm being buried myself, and I'm trying desperately to claw my way out of the ground. Sometimes, I prefer to lay quietly underground, even though it's hard to breathe. And sometimes I feel so golden and glittery that no darkness can touch me. (For this category, I'm usually dancing, roller skating, or with children.)

One thing I know is that you can't control grief when it crashes over you like a tsunami. Grief doesn't care if you are in the middle of a performance, in a meeting, swimming in the ocean, baking cookies, or giving a lecture at a university. It comes whenever it comes, and there's nothing you can do about that but let it wash over you.

That's what makes it hard to operate in the regular world. I usually have to warn people that I am grieving, in case I need to rush out of the room sobbing.

I tell the kids, sometimes it's so overwhelming, so deeply painful, you fall to your knees doubled over, and you feel like it will never stop.

But it will.

It *will* stop, and you will stand up, wipe the tears from your face, and carry on.

But you can't stop it, and you can't rush it.

It will take as long as it takes.

And it takes a long long time. Maybe forever.

It is generally agreed upon that there are five stages of grief: denial, anger, bargaining, acceptance. But it's not a neat path where you can say, okay, two weeks for denial, two weeks for anger, two weeks for bargaining... no. The stages are not sequential, but more waves. You move back and forth between all the stages, up and down, around and around, then back to Stage 1 when you thought you had passed Stage 5. Instead of steps, think of the 5 stages as a ninja warrior course.You leap from stage to stage, clinging for dear life as the thing you are clinging to moves around, gets slippery, and you have to find ways to hang on or you drop and start over again.

In my years of belly dancing, I did dances at the deathbeds of many an elderly people. I also danced at more weddings than I could ever count. But it just occurred to me, why aren't divorce parties a part of our culture? If they ever do become a part of our culture, they should definitely employ belly dancers. Think about it: we have rituals for marriage, rituals for death, rituals for birth, but no ritual for divorce.

When I was pregnant with my daughter, I had a baby shower that was also a ritual. My friend running it, Laura, had all the women sit in a circle and each woman said their name and "I accept Marci into my life as a mother." It sounds simple, but for me it was powerful. These were my circus and dancing friends, and we had spent many years together performing and celebrating life. Now, I was changing forever — I was becoming a mother — and something about saying those words helped me and my dear friends accept this new, very important transition in my life. At my tiny wedding, my very close ones were there to witness me go from one single person to a married person and a family. The ritual proclaimed to the world that we were dedicated to each other forever, devoting our lives to one another and our children.

Now that has changed again. I am different now. I am a single mother. That means it is me alone steering the ship for the children. When they need comfort, or I need comfort, support, anything, I no longer have my significant other. It's just me.

I think a divorce ritual, with belly dancing, would be helpful.

So maybe a funeral ritual would say, "I accept Marci in my life as a single mother, without a father, and without a partner. Just Marci." And of course there should be a gorgeous gown, and a very tall tiered cake.

Chapter 22
Single Mom Extraordinaire

I just met one of my besties, Cristie, for an impromptu quick cup of tea after morning drop-off. I broke my cardinal rule about going into public dressed in my sweats, and of course I ran into many people I knew, but at least I had curled my hair and put on lipstick, so it wasn't a *total* disaster. This is not a cultural standard, but my own standard. This is New England—NO ONE wears lipstick, curls their hair, or wears colors, except for me.

But for me, no matter where I am, life just seems better when I have my hair curled and my lipstick on. Add a colorful dress, tutu, sparkling boots, and how can life be anything but bright and happy?

But if you know me, you know the past couple of years have been full of tragedy that I'm still processing. Tutus and sparkle boots help for some reason! I don't know why, they just do. Try them!

Anyway, Cristie told me about her crazy week because her husband is injured and can't get out of bed. She has to do everything and her week sounds like my life: organize the kids, the house, drive the kids everywhere, who usually have to be across town at the exact same time—8am drop off for multiple kids at schools 20 miles apart; 4pm pickup for everyone… breakfast every morning, dinner every night, help with homework, laundry for multiple people, fix cell phones, handle the car, handle the leaky faucet, grocery shop, toilet paper, paper towels, care for five pets, water the greenhouse, this child needs new bras, this child has somehow run out of pants that fit him....

I have become a tech wizard. I fix computers and crashed internets, I program remote controls, and repair broken printers. I clean the house, walk the dogs, take care of the gardens, handle leaky faucets and frozen pipes and call the handyman if I can't defrost frozen pipes myself. All this on top of caring for the children, teaching belly dance, and writing and substitute teaching every day possible while I look for a job.

Being a divorced single mom feels a lot like Burt in Mary Poppins, a one-man band, playing an instrument strapped to every part of his body. That's me, trying to orchestrate our lives and make a symphony of beautiful music all on my own.

And like Burt, I do it with a cheery smile and a wink, because... well.... why be a grouch about it?

There are magical moments where I dance with gusto across rooftops with my broom, my face and hands black with dirt and soot. There are moments where I grab the kid's hands and we disappear into a painting, to dance with penguins or ride carousel horses that take off and fly, as we marvel at the beauty all around us. There are moments where we laugh so hard we float to the ceiling and can't remember what it feels like to be on the ground.

And there are moments where we stand on the ground with tears running down our faces as the magic flies away.

But then we make our own magic by throwing our dream kites into the air, running to make them fly.

If there's one thing we have learned these past few years, it's that we make our own magic! No one else will make it for us.

My brother, Carlos, came to visit me recently. After helping me drive kids all over, bringing in firewood and taking out the trash, he looked around my life and said, "I think one of the hardest parts of being a single mom, besides the obvious part of doing everything, would be the lack of emotional support. The buck stops with you. You don't have anyone to take care of you when you don't feel good, to put their arms around you at the end of a tough day and tell you everything is going to be alright, to talk to about the kids, sharing their triumphs and struggles. It's just you."

I nodded sadly. "True."

Then he grabbed me in a headlock and gave me a noogie by rubbing my head with his knuckles. Even though I'm 50 and he's 60, and we should be past this phase. But we're not. He's my brother, and pre-programmed to mess with me.

And weirdly, just having my brother put into words one of the hardest parts of being a single mom, helped in some way. I hadn't thought of it before, I was just running from thing to thing, grabbing and holding, balancing everything so nothing crashes to the ground and gets broken.

I'm lucky that I have my brother, my friends, my sisters, and so much support around me. But I also have a secret weapon. His name is Don. I have a great handyman who is a superhero in the disguise of a salty New Englander who doesn't say the letter R in any word. He knows my house inside and out because he worked on it long before I moved in. He is the type of handyman who takes photos of my broken pipes and sends them to me, telling me why they were broken, even if I'd rather not know. Lord knows, I don't need to see photos of my broken sewage pipes. But these days, I have learned that it's good to know.

Don't turn away, Marci! Knowledge is power, and not knowing doesn't change the truth. If your pipes are broken and covered in crap, don't look away! Fix them!

So I look at the photos, say, "Yuck," and know that the pipes in the house are not a big unknown mystery. They are laid out in an organized way that makes everything run efficiently. My handyman knows how they work, and now I know how they work.

In addition to being able to fix anything and everything from stone fences to squirrel nests, ice dams to water heaters, Don collects old maps. He scans the locations of ancient porches and sledding hills with his metal detector, anywhere where things fall out of pockets, finding pre-revolutionary war belt buckles, rare coins, and all sorts of cool things. I love seeing his treasures. He brings them over in bags with papers telling about their history and I call the kids to come see the Indian head pennies and satchel buckles from the 1700's.

Yesterday he showed up with a 5,000 year old arrowhead he recently found. 5,000 years!! If that doesn't put things in perspective I don't know what will! And a couple of weeks ago, Don gave me a DVD to watch with the kids. It was a news segment about a shipwreck off New England and the 5 divers who trained for months to dive more than 500 feet to explore the wreck that killed more than 200 people off the coast of Boston in the 1800's. How extraordinary is that? My handyman is one of five people in the world who has dived to that shipwreck! In a cool twist, the news segment also had a bit with another friend of mine, Dan Finamore, Curator of Maritime Arts at the Peabody Essex Museum. He spoke about the shipwreck, which was a legendary calamity until the Titanic sunk a few years later and took over the title as worst tragic shipwreck.

Cristie likes to tell the story of the first time she met my handyman. It was many years ago on Valentine's Day, so of course I was wearing a red tutu and antennas with furry blinking hearts on them. Don was talking to me in his salty-no-nonsense-way, while I nodded my head in my sweet-very-full-of-nonsense way. She said she was very amused watching me answer the door in my tutu and antennas, and Don didn't bat an eye but started telling me about my pipes, while I stood there nodding and blinking.

Cristie is the queen of amusing observations, and there's no one more gifted in recounting hilarious anecdotes.

Don has been our superhero now for almost a decade. He came over and hung drapes for my parents when they arrived, limped to my door when he saw an ambulance pull up to my house, and stood quietly with his back to me, as I broke down sobbing a few weeks later while telling him I no longer needed a walk-in Jacuzzi tub for my Dad because he didn't make it. When my sobs quieted, he kept on talking about the project. A few weeks later, when my ex left, he came over to remove all furniture and all memories of my ex. And now all these years later, he helped me and the kids move into our new home, hanging chandeliers and artwork and fixing things. When I told him I couldn't afford to fix the floors in my new house, he offered to loan me the money.

So I have to go pick up my manuscripts, teach Harry Potter class, make cookies to sell at the school play this weekend, pick up my son, make dinner, pick up my daughter... the usual Thursday evening.

Single Mom Extraordinaires do it all! But it sure helps to have the helpers: brothers, sisters, friends, and an amazing handyman.

And you can bet I'll be doing it in my sparkle boots.

Chapter 23
Crowns

I'm tired of being in pain all the time. I'm tired of wearing a crown of thorns. They pierce my skin and they never stop hurting. I want to switch my crown of thorns into a crown of butterflies. Did you know that a group of butterflies is called a kaleidoscope? Did you know that when caterpillars are transforming into butterflies they turn into liquid? That might be where I'm at right now. I feel completely liquefied, pretty mushy, unformed, and there's not a darn thing I can do to force myself to rise faster.

If you open a chrysalis, if you try to make the butterfly open its wings before its ready, it will break, it will die. You can't rush it. Sounds a lot like grief. There's no shortcut. It will take as long as it takes. And when enough time has passed, it seems you should be healing, as life goes on all around you, that is when you are in the middle of a swamp so deep you can't see your way out. You don't know how you will get to the other side. You have no choice but to trust that eventually you will see light, and you will know which direction to go in to enter the light. But right now, it's dark.

And it feels like I'm wearing a crown of thorns, a crown because it is my thoughts that torture me, reliving dark moments over and over again on an endless loop of pain. I want my crown to stop hurting. I want my crown to flutter with light and colorful wings.

But what about this? Sometimes I feel like I might have a crown of crows.

After my ex left, Kim took me on a hike through the woods. We went up a hill and sat down on a large rock overlooking the ocean. She told me to scream, primal screams. I shook my head. "No thank you." I'd rather not scream right now, I'm still cartwheeling through space. She said she'd do them with me. She opened her mouth and screamed. I tried to join her, even though I didn't want to, and within seconds, I collapsed sobbing on her lap, while she rubbed my back. She said, "That's the whole point, you know. To break through that wall holding in your grief and release it."

I couldn't answer, so I just lay there pooled in heart-wracking soul-shaking sobs feeling her hand on my back, her legs supporting me, the air filled with the scent of the salty sea and evergreen trees.

It seems appropriate that a group of crows is called a "murder," right? The old me is gone forever, crushed in a brutal way. This is a new me, a heartbroken me, a soul staring straight into the dark side of life, the sad side, the side of loss and the realization that the world I thought was beautiful and safe, may not be so nice after all. But then again, here I am. Let me say that again, here I am: honest, loyal, true, loving. Maybe it wasn't me that was murdered. Maybe it was my life full of lies, liars, and false promises. Now I hold my head high in the light of truth and integrity, and that feels a lot like wearing a crown of butterflies. Light and free. So maybe the screaming "murder" of crows isn't me releasing my grief, maybe it's the releasing of darkness, toxic people, and liars.

And maybe the world actually is nice. Like a kaleidoscope, the patterns and colors keep changing depending on my perception. Did you know that butterflies do not move their wings up and down, but in figure eights, or infinity symbols? That's just like I move my body when I dance. They are so fragile and fleeting, changing and moving. Fluttering their wings in the pattern of eternity. Native Americans believed butterflies were loved ones who had passed, making a connection, reminding us that beautiful souls are both temporal and eternal at the same time.

Soul growth, transcendence and transformation can be messy business. Just ask a butterfly. Or me.

Chapter 24
How Divorce is Like Chitty Chitty Bang Bang

I've been divorced for two weeks, and the battle wounds are not healed yet. There are many many loose ends to sort out, but the relief of having the battle over is surreal. Even more surreal is accepting my new title of divorcee...

Hello Darling, I am a 'divorcee.'

Actually, I don't know if I like this new title.

I mean, it does sound *kind of* fabulous, glamorous, and slightly scandalous, like I should be strutting the world in a big hat with feathers like any self-respecting divorcee. *"I'm on Husband Number Five."*

But on the other hand, it sounds sad, like I've survived some terrible battle and been changed forever, which is true too. Sigh. I'd rather not be called "Marci the Divorcee." If you must call me that, at least call me "Marci the Darling Divorcee." Yes that's better. But if I could choose any title this morning, I would choose to be called **Lady Scrumptious.**

Where did I come up with such an adorable name you ask?

I'm not sure, but I believe I picked it up from the epic film, *Chitty Chitty Bang Bang*. The main character is named Truly Scrumptious and her father is Lord Scrumptious. Really. Now if that's not the best character name on the planet, I don't know what is. Except a close second is another character from *Chitty Chitty Bang Bang*, the eccentric inventor: Caractacus Pott, which is a wonderful play on words because it can be shortened to "crackpot," which I love because never a day goes by when I don't feel like a crackpot. But 'crackpot' doesn't evoke the same delightful images as Lady Scrumptious, which makes me think of cream puffs and everything delicious, while "crackpot" makes me think of a messy-haired wild inventor creating new magical things... and truly I am both.

And how's this for an epic soup of creativity?

The screenplay for the film was co-written by Roald Dahl, based on a book by Ian Fleming called Chitty Chitty Bang Bang: The Magical Car. Really. So I wouldn't be out of line to sip a martini while wearing a terrycloth playsuit ala Sean Connery in James Bond, on my way to the chocolate factory? I'm in!

Darlings, divorce is so much like the story of *Chitty Chitty Bang Bang*!

Listen to this:

In the film, there are two characters, Baron and Baroness Bomburst, who hate children and employ a 'childcatcher' to capture and imprison them. The townspeople must hide their children in a grotto in order to keep them alive.

Sounds like the divorce process, right?

Besides the obvious destruction to families and children caused by divorce, there is also the destruction of our inner children—the childlike parts of us, the parts that look at the world with wonder and curiosity, marveling at all its magic. Divorce relentlessly pounds the fun, wonder, and beauty out of everyone involved, leaves a broken painful mess in its wake. So when it comes to divorce, flying cars are very handy. I mean, which of us hasn't dreamed of owning a flying car, especially when sitting in traffic, or divorce court?

I highly recommend that when things get rough, close your eyes and call your imaginary flying car to pick you and your children up so it can take you all somewhere wonderful.

And OMG, if you read the list of songs in the musical version of *Chitty Chitty Bang Bang*, it's a veritable guide to the divorce experience:

"You Two" (You meet your future ex)

"Toot Sweets" (Courtship)

"Think Vulgar" (You find out he has been lying all along)

"Act English" (Stiff upper lip and all that, in order to keep your family together)

"Hushabye Mountain" (If you don't speak your truth, marriage goes really well)

"Come to the Funfair" (Things aren't what they appear)

"Me Ol' Bamboo" (Use a bamboo walking stick to help your marriage limp along)

"Posh!" (Retail therapy is always helpful)

"Chitty Chitty Bang Bang" (Call in the flying car to take your mind away when things get tough)

"Truly Scrumptious" (Time to speak your truth—which feels delicious)

"Vulgarian National Anthem" (A last ditch attempt to keep you in the marriage to snuff out your magic)

"The Roses of Success" (You stand in your magic—aka truth and integrity and kick him out)

"Chu Chi Face" (This is the song description—no kidding: The Baron and Baroness hate children, and as the couple profess their love for one another, the Baron is simultaneously trying to kill his wife through equally barbaric means, yet his attempts always fail. Despite the obvious attempts on her life, the Baroness completely overlooks the fact that her husband wants her dead, even after he triggers an axe to fall on her head, a barbed spike to fall from the chandelier, and a trap door to open under her. The song is a humorous take on couples who maintain a façade of undying love, but have secretly grown to despise one another.)

"Doll on a Music Box" (Everyone knows dolls on music boxes are pretty but very rigid and they can't go anywhere— destined to turn in circles in the same spot forever—a lot like a marriage built on lies... or the divorce process—turning in circles, never going anywhere)

"Chitty Flies Home" (When you finally realize the soul-sucking "child catching" nightmare that is the divorce process, you stop fighting, call in your flying car and get the hell out—

let your ex have whatever-- keep your children and your soul, take a leap of faith out of the toxic swamp)

Voila! Incredible how similar *Chitty Chitty Bang Bang* is like divorce.

Chapter 25
Look for the Rainbows

After my father died, and my husband left, the kids and I were reeling in grief and bone-burning loss. We always took big trips over spring break to see the people we love in various places, so in a typical year we would go to Orlando to see my niece, Austin to see my sister, Utah to see my parents and other sister, etc... This year, the Muir Woods popped into my head. I felt like it would be healing to all of us to walk in an ancient forest among the redwoods. I didn't know why, but it seemed right. I have two dear friends who live in Northern California, Zar and Tanya, and we decided to go visit them along with the woods. Zar, Tanya and I couldn't be more different as people. Zarafshan appropriately means sparkle in Hindu, and Zar is definitely sparkly in a different way than me. She grew up in Pakistan and speaks seven languages. She is smart and gorgeous, bawdy and hilarious. She is a mathematics and business whiz who now lives with her husband and two adorable wild red-headed children near San Francisco. Tanya is one of the most gentle, kind, selfless, loving people I've ever met, and really really good at organizing. When we backpacked pre-internet, it was Tanya who went to the payphones at the train stations to find us places to stay, while Zar and I watched the backpacks, making up names for ourselves like Peaches and Cream and Kibbles and Bits, while giggling at our own ridiculous jokes.

The kids and I flew into San Francisco, and I had made a dinner reservation at some fancy restaurant. One of the things I was sad about when my ex left was no more fabulous date nights. My ex was a foodie and delighted in researching amazing restaurants and we had many epic transformational wine-filled nights together.

I decided I would have to continue these journeys on my own with the kids, but upon arrival, it occurred to me that the kids don't really enjoy sitting at fancy dinners, and they'd rather have mac-and-cheese or pizza than truffle mushroom risotto. And they don't drink wine. And I realized, I too would rather eat pizza with the kids and laugh and play than go sit at a restaurant for fancy food.

Excellent revelation— I cancelled our reservation and we had pizza.

So we went to wine country on my birthday with Zar and Tanya and the kids. As we drove through the gorgeous vineyards, we saw not one, not two, but SEVEN RAINBOWS! SEVEN!!!! On my birthday. It seemed like a personal message to me that everything was going to be okay, even though I couldn't imagine how.

I had not seen a rainbow at this point in about 15 years. One day in 2002, skiing with my ex, I had an epic rainbow day where I saw so many rainbows I thought the rapture was happening. It looked like I was skiing on rainbow glitter because it reflected in the snow. A few years before that, Kim and I had gone to visit my ancestral castle on the Isle of Skye in Scotland and saw 13 rainbows in one day. We kept trying to find the pot of gold at the end, but all we did was laugh our asses off as we chased them all over. Which I guess was the real pot of gold—our laughter and love for each other.

Flash forward, and it had been many many years with no rainbows.

But here I was, on my 49th birthday, grieving so much loss, and I was screaming in the car. Yelling for Zar to pull over so I could take a picture. My daughter said, "Mom, stop screaming, you're scaring Zar and Tanya." I tried to tone it down, but I was high on rainbows! What can I say? I get excited when I see a rainbow.

Later, I told my friend Courtney about the day, and asked her if it was extraordinary that I screamed when I saw a rainbow like someone else might scream seeing Mick Jagger.

She quietly said, "Maybe."

I said, "Well, what do you do when you see rainbows?"

She said, "I might smile to myself. I might take a picture, but I don't scream and jump up and down."

Hmmm, okay. So maybe I was overreacting, but I truly madly deeply love rainbows. The next day we went to the Muir Woods, and guess what?

We saw so many more rainbows. They were shooting everywhere through the woods. They were shooting off the kids like cat whiskers, shooting through the trees, dancing in my hair like jewels. Everything in that forest looked like it was glowing and unfurling, wrapping me in beauty.

It was like being dropped in a fairy wonderland: the glowing colors, the furling fronds, the flowers looked like they were blooming right in front of my eyes — it was that powerful. I had my Rumi book of poetry with me, and I read lines of poetry while we walked among these massive gorgeous trees, the smell of redwood and moss everywhere, neon green ferns gracefully waving at our feet, as I thought, "I don't need a house, I could live right here next to these magnificent trees and be very happy." I still feel high from that day a year later!

AND we saw ANOTHER RAINBOW the next day. This one was like a massive pour through the rainclouds in such vibrant colors—it was the first time I saw the purple in a rainbow so thick and bright. Now that I think about it, that particular rainbow looked like a RAINBOW WATERFALL out of the sky!

We were on a quest to see the Jules Feiffer waterfall in Big Sur, as waterfalls are another thing that heals my soul. We drove a long way on winding roads above steep ocean cliffs, surrounded by one of my favorite smells — pine trees and ocean mixed together. We got to the waterfall, hiked down the path, and looked with excitement, only to find the waterfall was a small trickle. The kids were exasperated with my quest to see the trickle, but we are still laughing about it a year later, and after the trip was over, Annabelle said it was her favorite part. She loved driving through the dark in the rain on ocean cliffs, through farmlands, listening to Nancy Drew on audio book while the rain pelted our car — after seeing the massive rainbow of course.

Rainbows, waterfalls, and poetry are all things that heal me, but the best part was spending time with Zar and Tanya, Annabelle and Henry, creating memories that can never be taken away, no matter what we go through in life.

And when we came home, I decided to start teaching a Rainbow Unicorn class at my kids school as an after-school class, which became so popular that it's now my summer camp and I'm still teaching it. The kids and I show up in glitter rainbow clothing, and I can completely indulge my overenthusiasm for rainbows and all things magical with tiny humans who share my enthusiasm.

I hope my kids take away that when we need support, it's all around us, in the people we love, in the trees and the sea, in waterfalls and rainbows — we just have to open our eyes.

Chapter 26
Helping the Kids

My daughter says, "People don't understand how hard divorce is on the kids!"

I answer, "*Everyone* knows divorce is hardest on the children, but no one knows how to truly help."

Divorce is really hard on children, and divorce court is set up to make it even worse.

In my own experience as a Mom and educator, I have found the most powerful way to support and help children through trauma is to be an example of healthy coping strategies in your words and actions. It's called 'modeling,' but not the kind where you pose in front of cameras. In this version, you are 'modeling' exemplary behavior for your children. You can't control your emotions, but you can control your words and actions. And believe me, I know it's hard to act kindly towards someone who has betrayed and harmed you and your children. It can feel like chewing broken glass, but do it anyway. That doesn't mean you won't break down sobbing or lose your kind words on occasion. That's okay—it's human and the kids should see that too, so they know it's all part of the process. It's healthy for them to see you can break down crying, then you wipe your tears and carry on.

The kids are looking to us, the adults, to show them how to cope.

In the psychology world, therapists say that children view divorce like death, because it really is the death of the family they thought they'd have forever. That means they will go through the grieving process as if it actually is a death: denial, anger, bargaining/anxiety, sadness, acceptance. And the grieving process isn't usually quick. It can take years for everyone to process the death of their family.

My daughter feels that the kids should have a voice in the divorce process, and that their opinions should be respected. She says it's the kids who get hurt the most, so why don't they get to clearly say what makes the whole thing less painful for them?

I agree.

She heard so many horror stories from other kids who were forced against their will into therapy and relationships with harmful toxic parents, so she dug in her heels and said no. She would decide and declare what she needed.

Here's what helped my kids:

1. **The #1 way to help your children is to Model Resilience.** Think about how you truly want your children to handle life's blows, and then become it. I know it can be really hard to act with kindness and grace to someone who has betrayed you, but you have to transcend, rise above it, and try to act with kindness and generosity while maintaining fierce boundaries. If you can do this, your kids have a better chance of making it out of the nightmare with coping skills and excellent boundaries that will serve them the rest of their lives.

2. **Make a Mission Statement:** The day after my ex left, the kids and I pulled out a magic marker and created our own mission statement about what we wanted our home to be like with the three of us: creative, fun, lot's of laughter, light and love, and of course, dance parties and pillow fights.

3. **Trusted Listeners on the Outside:** Encourage your children to talk to trusted adults *that aren't you* so they can have someone outside the family as support. The trusted adults are there only to LISTEN, not to advise. And the kids get to choose their listeners, as long as they aren't making things worse.

4. **Therapy or No Therapy?** Don't *force* the kids into therapy. Let them know it's available to them when they are

ready. Therapy can be amazing, but it can also be really harmful, depending on the therapist. Let your kids take the lead on this, and if they ask to go to therapy, ask trusted friends for referrals. Make sure to have a therapist who has actually been positive and helpful. After their first session, your children should emerge feeling more empowered and stronger. If they don't, fire that therapist and keep looking. It took three years for my daughter to find a therapist that wasn't harmful to her. She found one she loves and now she chooses to go every week. My son saw a therapist in the heat of everything.

5. **The Kids Have Rights!** The children should be held up above the divorce battle. They deserve to have their own rights, to voice where they feel safe and want to spend the majority of their time. Maybe they want to split time with their parents 50-50, maybe 80-20, but it should be about the kids, not the parents.

6. **Banana Splits Support Group**: my daughter went to school feeling embarrassed about her family situation, so she decided to start her own peer-run divorce support group at her school, calling it Banana Splits. She asked her school counselor to silently oversee it. They started meeting once a week to talk about their experiences in their own words, without adults telling them how they should or shouldn't feel. Kids started calling her for support when they were struggling with divorce issues, and helping others through the process has helped her heal.

7. **Fill the House With Positive Affirmations:** I bought stickers that said, "You are Beautiful" and put them on every mirror in my house to remind all of us. Also, we all wrote down words that reflected our values and taped them up all over: love, light, abundance, generosity, kindness…

8. **Allow for Rewinds:** we all have moments we wish we could take back. In our household, we actually can! We call them Rewinds, and if someone says something they don't mean, has a freak out, a meltdown, whatever, they can ask for a Rewind and we all nod and carry on as if it didn't happen. No one gets grounded or sent to their rooms. It's bizarrely effective

at keeping peace in the house and helping the kids understand that sometimes people lose their cool, but as long as you recognize it and center yourself as quickly as possible, it's okay.

9. **Scheduled Check-Ins**: I felt like I needed to check in with my kids constantly about how they were feeling. My daughter told me she didn't like being asked all the time because it hurt too much, so we made a plan that I would ask them once a week for an update on their emotions, and other than that, I wouldn't bring it up. Of course **they** were free to bring it all up anytime, but I wouldn't. It made the house feel safer for them, a place where they didn't have to worry about talking about painful things they weren't ready to discuss.

10. **Glitterbomb**: I love to Glitterbomb my kids by pointing out what is magical and joyful about them. (This term comes from the amazing Star Monroe—if you don't know her, look her up! She rocks!) They feel seen when I tell them, "I'm so proud of you for…" I'm amazed at how these words transform energy. My daughter is a Type A person who works really hard. It makes her really happy when I say, "I'm so proud of you and how hard you are working, your beautiful writing, your kindness towards your little brother, for bringing up the trash cans." And for my son, who calls himself a "Type B" meaning he'd rather lie in bed all day eating chocolate and playing video games while his sister is running the world. To my son, I say, "I'm so proud of you and your big heart, your compassion, your love of animals, babies, old people, bringing in the trash cans." All these things are things I expect my teenagers to do, but they love it when I tell them, "I see you. You are doing a great job.".

11. **Glitterbomb 2**: Occasionally, I randomly shout out "Glitterbomb!" and stand on a chair with a bottle of glitter. I ask the kids to tell me something recent that made them feel proud. "I'm proud of myself for being scared to get on a boat, but getting on it anyway; for raking all the leaves in my yard, for being kind to my baby sister, for getting an A on my history test…" They shout it out and then run by me while I sprinkle

glitter on their heads. If they don't want glitter, I'll just throw it in the air and we can watch it sparkle together as it falls to the floor.

12. **Midnight Margaritas**: My kids LOVE it when I yell MIDNIGHT MARGARITAS and blast music in their room after they've gone to bed. They come running down the stairs to the kitchen where I fill up big pink margarita glasses with popcorn and we play a few rounds of a card game and dance around the kitchen and the dining room table. It's twenty minutes of pure exquisite fun, just the three of us, and it's very healing and bonding.

13. **Look for the Miracles**: Part of "modeling resilience" means pointing out the miracles all around us, from the perfection of a single pink blossom, the golden light shining though an autumn tree, the sun making the snow glitter like diamonds, the changing light of the sky, the fog… just a quick, "Wow, look at the pink sky!" can work wonders. It teaches the children to notice the miracles which is a gift that can see them through rough times, even when you aren't around.

Chapter 27
Grandparents Guide to Divorce

Divorce is awful for everyone involved as the family dynamic shifts and changes under your feet like a dilapidated carnival funhouse. But grandparents are in a unique position to steady the shifting ground. Divorce is an opportunity for grandparents step into the role of Sanctuary. Keep your arms open wide and loving for your child, your child-in-law, and most of all, your grandchildren. Be the trusted listeners your grandchildren can call, knowing they can safely talk, cry, yell, and you will listen and not take sides. You are Switzerland: beautiful, gorgeous, with warm milk and cookies and only positive loving words coming out of your mouth. I know it can be hard to know what to do in divorce. There is no guide that advises grandparents on their role in divorce, so I have created one, and here it is:

1. STAY OUT OF IT! Remember, if you take sides, you are adding to the family's trauma, pouring salt on a very painful wound.

2. **Be Unconditional Love for *Everyone*.**

3. **Go Straight to the Grandkids** — Here's your script: "We love all of you and hope for the best outcome. We are going to let the adults figure out their issues and we are going straight to the grandchildren." Be there for them, love and support them, and don't take sides against either of their parents.

4. **Don't Bash Your Daughter/Son-in-law:** Here is another script you can use when your son is bashing his wife and the mother of his children: "I know you are hurting, but we love you *and* our daughter-in-law. We don't want to hear any

negativity or insults from either of you. We are here to help the grandchildren, you adults can work out your own issues." Then, redirect, "Have you seen any good movies lately? Or read any good books?" Redirect the conversation towards positive subjects that don't involve insulting or talking trash about anyone."

5. **Do not threaten, bully, litigate, or hire your own lawyers to add fuel to the fire. (**See Rule #1)

6. **How Can We Help?** Look around for ways to make the divorce process less painful for everyone. Ask if you can take the kids to school, bring over groceries, bouquets of wildflowers, drop them on the porch. Be a warm safe place for the entire family, which I hear is the best part of being a grandparent. (This won't work if you are threatening, bullying and attacking their mother. Again, see Rule #1.)

7. **Switzerland.** If it is your child who lied and cheated, don't make excuses for him or blame the innocent partner. (See #1.)

8. **Small Gestures.** Maintain a loving relationship with both parents. Send *loving* texts, gratitude letters, supportive messages to BOTH parents and the grandkids. "We are here for you. We love all of you. You are doing great!" (Again, this won't work if you take sides.)

I remember when I was a teenager and my older siblings were all married. One day my older sister had a fight with her husband, just as they were about to drive over to our house for a birthday party. She called my Dad and told him to send the husband away when he arrived, which my Dad did. I said, "Dad! When she married him, he became your son and my brother. He has as much a right to be here as she does, and just because they have a fight, you can't turn him away. You have to stay out of it." My Dad was an incredible human being. He agreed with me. He called my sister and told her he was staying out of it and not to involve him again. He called my brother-in-law and apologized, telling him to come back. That's called being a good father-in-law and grandparent.

Another sister is a grandparent to ten little ones! She has three sons, and there is sometimes friction with the in-laws. My sister, who is a bossy prickly Virgo, always meets the friction with love and kindness, because she puts the grandchildren and the family first. She will call me and talk about it, trying to understand where the daughter-in-law is coming from. She never holds her boys in an exalted state as angels— she knows they can be difficult, so she stays neutral and loving. As a result, she has a wonderful relationship with her entire group.

My girlfriend is a first-time grandparent to a toddler, and last night she sadly shared that her son and daughter-in-law were splitting after ten years together. No one lied or cheated, they just didn't want to be romantically together anymore. She said, "I told my daughter-in-law that she is still my daughter and she is always welcome at our home anytime for any amount of time." There is such good will between all the parties involved. I listened, and wished I had the same experience. I didn't.

It is my fervent hope that grandparents can understand that if they take sides, they will be inflicting harm on their grandchildren which makes a traumatic situation worse. If you are aggressively attacking your daughter-in-law, filing your own lawsuits to make things worse, secretly hiring your own lawyers to sit in on meetings so you can strategize against the other spouse, and sticking your nose where it doesn't belong— you are the wind blowing on a raging forest fire. I know this from personal experience. I called my in-laws when I discovered my ex was cheating, thinking they would come to me and the kids in kindness. Instead, they went to their son, told him to immediately withdraw our money from our bank accounts, and started a string of abusive, threatening texts towards me. They tried to bully me, attacked me over and over again, until I had to call the police to keep the peace. The kids and I came home one day and found a letter in the mailbox stating that the grandparents were suing us. WTF? Who sues their own grandkids? Then, in another devious twist, I couldn't figure out why my ex always had two lawyers with him at divorce meetings. I asked him and he shrugged, dropping his head like he always does when he's lying. It took me a year to finally figure out that the second lawyer wasn't his— it was his Dad's. Now, I ask you, what grown middle-aged man with a law degree has his dad overseeing his divorce?

Do you think this behavior made the divorce less painful and provided warmth and safety for the grandchildren? It didn't.

So, that's a cautionary tale that leads back to Rule #1: Stay Out of It!

I lift my glass to all the Grandparents out there who choose to be a sanctuary, who look for ways to soothe the pain of divorce and make all the relationships as positive as possible. Cheers!

Chapter 28
Martini Club

I showed up at my Pilates class this morning wearing big sunglasses to help soften the Mahoney Brothers who were hammering away at my head. (For those of you unfamiliar with 1920's slang, the Mahoney Brothers are a cute way of saying I was hung over.)

In my usual state of over-sharing, I announced to my class that I was hung over and had barely made it to class while I stumbled around, pulling off my cozy Ugg boots and putting on my non-slip socks. Because there is a sock monster that lives in my sock drawer, I can *never ever* find matching socks. So today I was wearing one hot pink sock and one blue sock. They are the kind of socks that have a message on the toes, so when you are bending over to touch your toes, you can't help but read the message. My pink sock said, 'Be Happy' and my blue sock said, 'Be Healthy.' When I do Pilates, I spend a lot of time reading my socks, silently conversing with them, thinking "Ahhh, socks, if only it were that easy! If only I could read my sock that says 'Be Healthy' and wham! I would start craving salads with no dressing instead of hot cheesy pizza!

I would read 'Be Happy' and feel instantly cheery, forgetting all about the text I got last night from my ex that he had written for some woman he is wooing but accidentally sent to me! Ouch!

If I was a sock designer, my socks might say something like, 'Muffin Tops are gorgeous!' Or 'He's not worth it!' or "You are a goddess!"

When I laid on my machine and started rolling around which is my favorite part of Pilates, (who doesn't love a workout that is done while reclining? That's my favorite kind of exercise!) I couldn't help moaning, half in pleasure (muscles), half in pain (head). When we got onto our backs, the overhead lights glared right through my sunglasses. I asked our incredibly perky teacher to please lower the lights, and my whole class snickered. I lifted my head, "What? Those insanely bright lights aren't bothering anyone else?" They snickered again and JJ cheerfully dimmed the lights. See, I told you, even her name is perky.

So let me back up to how I got here—I can only blame one person, actually two, and they are called my Martini Club.

I have to tell you, those of you going through grieving and loss like me, or those of you just living life cool and breezy, everyone needs a Martini Club. And mind you, you don't have to drink martinis, or any kind of cocktail. In fact, none of us are big drinkers, and some of us order iced tea or coffee instead of the Hot and Dirty Martinis that we have proclaimed to be our signature drink, mostly because it's the only martini on the cocktail list at our local tavern. It's hot and spicy, and the cheery waitresses call us the "Hot and Dirty Girls," which send us into giggles every time they say it. We are about as far from hot and dirty as it's possible to get, unless you are referring to the fact that we might be hot from baking endless batches of cookies. Although I'm definitely dirty right now because I was carrying a huge bag of flour back to its shelf a few minutes ago and I accidentally threw it into the air, covering me and my entire kitchen in a dusting of flour. This delighted my dogs, who stared at me, then set to licking the floor before I could stop them, turning the flour dust into paste.

My dogs do love to challenge my non-existent household skills with their mess-making.

And don't ask me how I ended up throwing a giant bag of flour in the air. Somehow, it started to slip, and my instinct was to throw it up instead of let it drop. That's why my sister calls me Inspector Clouseau. When I bake at her house, she follows me around with a mop and a hot pad, grabbing falling cookie sheets from the counter and mopping up the flying cookie dough that ends up on the floor.

So yeah, I guess you could say we are hot and dirty, at least I am.

Last night the Martini Club texts started flying around till we found a time that worked for all of us and I walked over to the local tavern.

I love walking around my picturesque New England town in October. Candles glow in the windows of homes built in 1750, the air smells like burning wood and orange leaves swirl around like someone is throwing confetti on me or orange flour.

I live across from a historical house that hosts town events, so the streets this year are often filled with tiny children in witch hats carrying pumpkins in one hand and holding their mother's hand in the other. And I like to think about those hands and about holding my own daughter's hand and my mother's hand in the other in a matriarchal chain that has gone on for centuries. My mother has lost her mind after losing my father, probably a mercy so she doesn't remember he is not next to her after sixty years of never spending a night apart. I miss her, and when I see those little hands, I imagine I am holding my Mom's hand from across space and time as she's now in memory care near my father's burial site. I can see her wedding rings, the golden flower with the diamond in the middle, the perfectly manicured nails, and the soft scars that covered her left hand from the time she touched the stove as a child.

I miss her, and I'm grateful that I am walking to where I can literally reach out my hands and be held by the women in my Martini Club. I hate being so far from my family, but I love raising my kids with these women, who are endlessly inspiring as mothers. We are all as different as possible, but are aligned in parenting values and our sassy and irreverent personalities.

We were drawn together by having three daughters of the same age in the same class.

I met Cristie as soon as I moved here. She is the mom of three girls—two of which are in the same grades as my baby bunnies. Within a month of meeting her, she asked me to go take "witch pictures" in Salem. As the camera flashed and we paid $100 for the disc of photos, I thought "I really hope I get to be good friends with this woman or I'm going to have a bunch of photos with someone I don't even know." I need not have worried. When I saw the photos of her making her witch face next to me, and heard her constant stream of hilarious commentary on anything and everything around us, I knew we would be friends. Cristie actually has a PHD from Harvard in creating community (she would correct me and say ABD but I still count it), which is just so perfect because she's like a warm fireplace in a stone hut in the forest. Everyone is drawn to her warmth and easy going nature, and she has a knack for making everyone feel like she's their best friend.

The other Martini Club Member is Jacquie. I met Jacquie the night I organized a "Margaritas by the Sea" parent cocktail party for the 4th grade parents. One parent texted me and said, "Marci! How can I attend "Margaritas By the Sea" when I don't drink?" I replied, "Darling! You don't have to drink! I don't plan to drink that night! It just sounds more fun than "Orange Juice By the Sea" or "Guacamole By the Sea," although that sounds delicious. I love guacamole.

Anyway, Jacquie looked like an Ohio news anchor but was actually an actress and Ohio casting director, tall and thin with perfectly blown out hair, and a scarf tied neatly around her neck. She tossed her gorgeous hair when she talked and I overheard her say she had a house at Sundance. (Don't worry, I don't ALWAYS eavesdrop on other people's conversations, although as a writer and curious person, I can't help it.)

I interrupted her, "I grew up at Sundance. Where do you live?"

"We live on Buttercup Street next door to Gary…"

"Lamancha?" I interrupted again.

She stared at me. "How do you know Gary?"

"He went to high school with my Dad."

"You're kidding."

And so our friendship began. We had both been involved with the Sundance Film Institute and Festival—she attending and working in the film industry; me working in the Institute office in Santa Monica and at the Festival in Park City for five years. I suppose it is kismet that the first place we invited Jacquie was to Salem to take…wait for it… witch pictures! We took the train from my house to Salem, so we wouldn't have to park. It was a warm day so I ended up carrying the heavy faux fur capes that the kids had all worn over their costumes. We took photos and Jacquie later said she didn't know us at all, so she had smiled pretty for the camera, but when she saw the photos, she loved that Cristie and I were making full wicked witch faces. She gleefully told us, "We have to go back! I make a really good witch face!" Jacquie is another one who is an expert at creating community. Her house is always filled with children, and she is devoted to making their world as beautiful as possible.

After our first night out for martinis, the three of us, as different as possible—the Ohio casting director, the Italian comic, and the Rainbow Fairy, we laughed so hard we decided to make it a weekly event.

Now, six years later, we are still discussing our kids, husbands, ex-husbands, entrepreneurial ideas (A purple ice skating rink! A kiosk in Salem selling witch capes! An Art center! A Girl Power Conference! A film casting company!), and everything in between. We spend Christmas Eve and the Fourth of July together, and after my ex left, it was Jacquie's husband and son who brought us a Christmas tree and set it up for us because I had never done it alone. When my father came to live with me, it was Jacquie's husband, the head of cardiology at the hospital, who swung by to check on my Dad and promptly called an ambulance. It was Jacquie's husband who came the last time, and hugged me as he said, "I know you want to care for him, Marci, but he's way past that point." And it was Jacquie's husband I called from the hospice, while I was pacing in the garden next to a statue of a child blowing bubbles, to say I wasn't sure we should be there. With his soft kind voice, he reassured me that we had made the right decision.

When my ex abandoned ship a few weeks later, Jacquie and Cristie brought flowers and hugs. And when my best friend's heart stopped beating 3,000 miles away, they swooped in and took over the kids so I could fly to be by her side and hold her hand; a hand I know as well as my own, the curve of her thumb, the graceful fingers, and hair follicles that look like stars in a dark sky.

The Martini Club meets in wild blizzards, heat waves, when the sidewalks are covered in pink blossoms or Munchkinland-colored leaves. We meet, order drinks and food, and talk and laugh and cry. In fact, last night I was telling them that as much as I want the divorce over, I'm scared for it to be over. It takes up so much of my mental space, that I'm afraid when it's over, I'll be left to think about losing my father and Kim in a much bigger tsunami way. Jacquie lost her father last Fall. She took my hand and squeezed it. "I can't accept my Dad is gone either," she said, and handed me her napkin to wipe the hot tears that were spilling down my face.

We couldn't be more different, but we adore each other. We are there for each other, and each of us knows that we stand by the other in any storm. I know their stories, their kids, their brothers and sisters and their parents. Over time, we have found things that really make us laugh. For example we have an affinity for furry balls, and we get endless delight out of cracking 7th grade level jokes about them, including furry ball puns, gags, and gifts.

We present each other with martini socks, and dish towels, and Christmas tree ornaments hand painted with martinis and our names.

Creating community and supportive friendships is key to surviving the slings and arrows of life, especially when those slings and arrows are carrying nuclear grenades with them. So, Dr. Marci is handing out a prescription to those of you out there who are dealing with darkness, to create your own Martini Club. Drink whatever you want, but remember everything tastes better in a fun glass with a cute umbrella and people who get you.

Chapter 29
Ten Commandments of Divorce

1. Be cheerful and charming and your world will brighten in unexpected ways! (Even when you want to throttle someone.)

2. Look for the miracles all around you: butterflies, a blooming flower, the smell of rain, the sparkle of sunlight on the ocean, your child's arms around you...

3. Be generous and kind, and you will feel beautiful and powerful.

4. Let the negative feelings wash over you, then turn to the light. Fill your life with so much beauty there's no room for the darkness.

5. Plan an extravagant trip with your kids—sell your jewelry to pay for it!

6. Once a month try something you have never tried before: flamenco dancing, cooking something new, kayaking, painting, cello, cartwheels, going to the opera...

7. Daily physical exercise in nature with a friend.

8. Don't be a Bitter Betty (You have no control over your ex, but you have total control over yourself, your actions, and what you choose to focus on.)

9. Turn away from the Path of Pain (Don't check his social media EVER!)

10. Don't let your mind torture you in the circles of hell—write up reminders all over your house with words that inspire you.

Chapter 30
Divorce in a Patriarchy (I Prefer Divorce in a Pastry-Archy)

Patriarchy? Does the Patriarchy still exist, you ask? I'll let you be the judge. So let's start with the fact that I just finished house hunting and started wondering why the big bedroom in every house is called the "Master." *Why?* Why isn't it called the "Mistress?" Or better yet, "Mistress Minx?" Or "Mistress Cream Puff?" I don't want to sleep in a "Master." I want to sleep in a "Mistress Minx" room with a bed shaped like a cream puff and a mattress as soft as a croissant. Maybe that's what Master Suites should be called" "Mistress Minx Cream Puff Rooms." It has a nice ring to it. Better than Master.

Another example: I received address labels today asking for donations to something, addressed to the "Head of Household" and naming my 13- year-old son. What the heck?

Another example: Last summer in Europe, two of our hotels had handwritten notes welcoming my teen son, Mr. Henry Howard and family. Gee thanks. I do believe it's Mom who is the Head of the Family, who planned the entire trip and paid for it, but go ahead, address your little cards to my teenage son who can't remember to wear shoes.

Another example: A few days ago, I renewed our family membership with the Trustees who protect and oversee all the nature reserves in Massachusetts and the membership came addressed to my son again, with his name as the primary member and me and my daughter listed in small letters as "Additional family members."

I mean, what are we, chopped liver?

Patriarchy and its ugly cousin, misogyny, is front and center in the world of divorce, and it's tripled when you are a stay-at-home Mom. When I was forced, kicking and screaming into the Divorce World, I was horrified as several different lawyers told me that family law says that neither parent is allowed to stay home. They don't care if it's in the children's best interest. They don't care if you have made a family decision that this is best for your particular circumstance. Nope. Both parents must work and you have to figure something out with the kids. Great. So now in addition to the kids being traumatized by the divorce, they have to figure things out on their own or with strangers to watch them.

I always told my ex that if I was going to stay home with the kids, I needed my own bank accounts and savings. He said, over and over, "That's ridiculous. I'll never leave you." And then, in a not-so-shocking twist, the ultimate middle-aged man cliché, he left. And here I am trying to find a way to support my children.

Now I'm lucky that I have a Bachelor's degree in English and a Masters degree in Education, so that must count for something in the paying world.

But hey! I just realized the names of the degrees are completely patriarchal as well!! Why are they called Bachelors and Masters and not "Bachelorettes" and "Mistresses?" Why does the word "Bachelorette" evoke images of drunk girls in boas screaming with their heads poking out of the ceiling of their limos? While the word "Mistress," well that just makes me think of a dominatrix with black leather and a whip.

Maybe BA should stand for BadAss? And instead of a Masters degree it should be a Mistress degree? But here we are back with the lady with black boots and a whip. As long as she's only whipping cream, I'm in. Add some strawberries and shortcake to that cream and I'll follow her anywhere.

And a Masters Degree should be renamed "Her Majesty's Degree." Yes. I like that.

So a really fun part of divorce was when my ex decided to depose me. For what? I never did anything that might require deposing. My ex's lawyer was female, at least I think she was, but the only way to tell was her name, which was Lisa. And I don't know a lot of men named Lisa. One of the first things this ugly-hearted lawyer asked me was, "What do you do all day?"

Every stay-at-home Mom loves this question since we wake up hitting the ground running, starting with laundry, breakfast for the kids, driving them to school, cleaning their rooms and the house, going to see them sing at school meeting, running forgotten items to school, going to pick up cleats, ballet slippers, the mandatory mouth guard, the pants that have gotten too small for the second time this month, then to the basketball game. Then it's home to make a snack, before picking up the other child and taking her to dance class, home to make dinner, back to pick up the dancing child, making another dinner for her before helping with homework, and if my eyes are still open at the end of the day, sitting down to write or return emails.

I shouldn't have to explain this to anyone, but I'm going to guess that lawyer wasn't a mother and thinks I sit around eating bon-bons all day, lounging in my feathered robes.

And now that I mention it, what exactly is a bon-bon? A pastry? Sounds adorable and delicious. Maybe it's time I tried some while I'm job-hunting in between caring for my kids and making a magical home for them.

Because if there's one thing we can all agree on, it's that a Pastry-archy is much better than a boring old stodgy Patriarchy.

It makes my head spin faster than a dessert tray in a bakery window, right? Which really isn't very fast.

Okay, it makes my head spin faster than a whirling dervish?

A whisk in a bowl of whipped cream?

A champion pole dancer?

(All of the above make more money than a stay-at-home mom, even the whipped cream.)

Several times during the divorce process, I was so horrified by the unjust decisions, that I wanted to march on City Hall to change laws for future divorcees, in order to protect them and the family. But on the other hand, I don't want to spend one more second in the world of Family Law — it's ugly, brutal, and full of pain and darkness; a toxic swamp where the only winners are the lawyers and their bank accounts.

And so I rise. Like warm dough on a sunny windowsill, like hot bread baked in a clay oven, like airy popovers, I rise.

Down with the Patriarchy! Up with the Pastry-archy!

And send Mistress Minx over here with her whip. My bonbons need some whipped cream to top them off. And by the way, for clarity, I'm not just job-hunting. Oh no. I'm planning to transform the world so my son and daughter can have a more just fair world, in which they can live and love. And maybe even someone to make them warm croissants on chilly mornings, so they can call their mother over to help eat them.

Chapter 31
Have You Ever Wrestled with a Rainbow Unicorn? How About a Hegelian Dialectic? Or an Ancient Text?

This morning I woke up to the scent of baking bread and literally floated down the stairs on a cloud of cinnamon. My house-guest, Almah Luce, is a stress-baker, meaning this morning, she made three loaves of braided cinnamon-sugar challah bread, black beans and rice and molasses cookies. Almah Luce is a blue-eyed eighteen-year-old girl, who is 6-feet tall, with waist-length blonde hair that is currently dyed red, She has a smattering of new piercings and tattoos, all appearing in the last few months since her mother left this world. Lulu's mother is/was my friend and teacher, Laura Kali, who left this world five months ago after a long battle with breast cancer. Lulu is heading to an East coast college on a full ride scholarship to be a physician's assistant, and she is currently quarantining in my home and baking in my kitchen.

And I am currently eating challah bread so light it is melting in my mouth as I write.

If you know my writing, you know I'm often thinking about the cruel dialectic of parenting. You give your heart and soul and life to these glorious souls, and if you do it well, they leave. The entire purpose of loving your children to the moon and back is so that their wings are strong enough to fly away!!

WHAT?? That seems insane! Which is why I added "cruel" to Hegel's dialectic.

But I think it works the other way as well, as I watch Lulu reach into the far recesses of my cupboards to bake anything and everything, and I finish a Facetime call with my own mother, who is currently living in a home in Utah, cared for by strangers, unable to see family due to Covid, except through Facetime. Since my father died a few years ago, my mother has entered a dream state, and during the call she was funny and making unusual neural connections that only she can understand, but when she saw a photo of my Dad, she burst into tears and said, "Oh is he with you? How is he?" Which made me burst into tears. I miss him too, and I miss her. My brothers, sisters and I tried to care for her ourselves after my father died, but when she broke her knee, neck and hip in quick succession, we finally surrendered to the fact that maybe her care was outside our scope. But I can't bear not being able to care for her myself, so maybe the daughter dialectic is devoting everything to caring for your mother, watching her disappear, by cancer or dementia, and loving her so deeply you want to wrap her up and carry her around with you, but knowing you can't.

I learned about Hegel's dialectic in a philosophy class at UCLA and it felt like a gong struck in my mind. I devoured books on the subject and explored it from every angle.

A year later, my poetry professor, Stephen Yenser, quoted similar thoughts by F. Scott Fitzgerald. In a 1936 Esquire article, Fitzgerald wrote an essay called "The Crack-up" which contained the following quotation: "…**the test of a first-rate intelligence is the ability to hold two opposed ideas in the mind at the same time, and still retain the ability to function**. One should, for example, be able to see that things are hopeless and yet be determined to make them otherwise. This philosophy fitted with my early adult life, when I saw the improbable, the implausible, often the "impossible" come true."

And quite frankly, I could write an autobiographical essay today and the title, "The Crack-up" would fit nicely, although I might change it to "The Crack-pot," as both are quite true. Meanwhile, I'll crack open another warm melted buttery slice of challah while I ponder.

For the past twenty years, I have thought a lot about the dialectic and its cruelty. I was researching various philosophies recently when I came across a third piece of the dialectic I had never learned.

What is it? Drum roll please...

SYNTHESIS!

What? Can this be true? How did I ever miss the third part? I thought I was left hanging with the conundrum of two opposing sides being true at the same time, and never the two should meet, but if this theory is true, in any dialectic there is synthesis!

What the hell does this mean?

According to the Oxford English dictionary, "In Hegelian philosophy, the final stage of dialectical reasoning, in which a new idea resolves the conflict between thesis and antithesis." "It is also noted that the dialectical process is not simply from thesis and antithesis to final synthesis; it is an eternal, open-ended spiral of development."

And again, what the hell does that mean? Are we on an endless loop of pain and suffering, like Dante's seven circles of hell, falling through the roaring fires of bone-burning loss, screaming for lost love?

Or is this spiral a gorgeous fiery goddess symbol, not endless pain but boundless love, and learning where that boundless love is found in loving and letting go, over and over again?

Or can both be true at the same time?

Jesus, I'm blowing my own mind.

But I do love a spiral and an infinity symbol, as they are the sacred shapes of belly dance. Nothing makes me feel more centered, empowered, and connected than belly dancing.

You can go back much further than Fitzgerald in ancient texts and find the same theme explored over and over. For example, there is a 2,000-year-old poem called "The Thunder: Perfect Mind," discovered in the gnostic manuscripts at Nag Hammadi, and it speaks in the voice of a divine feminine power that unites opposites. "I am knowledge and ignorance... I am strong and I am afraid... I am war and I am peace... I am the mother and the daughter..." (I just had a vision of a woman reciting the poem while someone belly dances. How gorgeous!)

The poem is a shining marvelous example of the quest of the human soul to make sense of this world, to unite opposites. It has inspired countless research and gorgeous art. Recently, the poem was the foundation of Sue Monk Kidd's current bestselling novel, "*The Book of Longings*," and just this morning I came across the poem in a beautiful Prada ad from 2010, directed by Jordan Scott and her father, Ridley Scott. I never knew Prada was tapping into ancient texts to make art.

After experiencing staggering heartbreak, I am constantly searching for people who have made it to the other side. Many spiritual teachers tell us not to run away from pain, but to run towards it, invite pain in and let it teach us its lessons. That sounds like a terrible idea, but maybe a beautiful idea too. I don't know, sounds a lot like a dialectic.

I shall take a bite of a molasses cookie and think about it. And in a lovely piece of synchronicity, my mom used to make molasses cookies all the time. She'd give us a little bowl of sugar to roll the balls of dough in and put on the cookie sheet. They were delicious, and for years I thought they were called "Alaska cookies." I think I was 15 when I finally realized they were called molasses cookies. My Dad and Henry's favorite joke involves some moles climbing out of a hole and the little one saying all he could see was "mole asses." Also Lulu's entire name is Almah Luce, which means "Light of the Soul."

At this point, the one thing I've learned is I don't know a damn thing, except maybe I know everything because I know nothing. Probably the only thing I know at the moment is Lulu makes a damn good molasses cookie.

And thinking about all of this feels a lot like wrestling with a rainbow unicorn, which coincidentally I just did.

So, to synthesize, we have dialectics, spirals, uniting opposites and knowing all can be true at the same time?

I guess we can establish I haven't figured out the synthesizing part yet.

What I do know is that for me, the one thing that makes life worth living, is Love (and cookies).

Loving deeply, while KNOWING that all great loves leave, in one way or another. Children grow up, lovers leave, soul mates die, mothers forget who you are, fathers die, furry teachers move on... (my daughter said I better clarify what a furry teacher is, so to clarify, a furry teacher is a pet); and even knowing that, knowing my bones will feel like they are on fire, maybe for years, knowing I will feel like I've been flung off a cliff into a dark abyss, knowing the lake of tears I will shed when that great love, that gorgeous shining soul leaves, I still choose love.

I always choose love.

I am the Mother and the Daughter.

I am strength and I am fear.

I am the wrestler of the Rainbow Unicorn.

Chapter 32
Divorce Divas Unite!

I love writing meaningful quotes on index cards and taping them up around my house. My bathroom mirror is so full of inspirational quotes it's nearly impossible to see myself! When people send me supportive messages or texts, I write them down and tape them up to remind myself, that when I'm feeling unlovable or like a failure or that all is lost and I'll never recover.

Here's a very important quote I found that is perfect for Divorce Divas. I wrote it down in red marker and pasted it front and center on my mirror:

1) Believe Patterns, Not Apologies
2) Don't Fall In Love With Potential
3) Believe ALL RED FLAGS!
4) KNOW YOUR WORTH!
5) Don't Lower Your Standards

1. I read "Believe patterns, not apologies" and said "Hallelujah Amen!" I am always so shocked when I learn someone is lying because I tend to believe people when they talk, assuming them to be honest. So when the silver-tongued serpent whispers his lies, I have to look at his actions, his patterns, and know that there lies the truth. Not in hollow words.

2. "Don't fall in love with potential"! How many of us do this? I would make up excuses for my ex, "Oh, well he's bitter and mean-spirited to people because he's stressed. He'll be

more kind when he's less stressed." Not true. People are who they are RIGHT NOW.

3. "Believe all red flags." Before we were even married, I caught my ex in a huge lie: for the entire two years of our passionate, romantic, intense courtship where we were planning our wedding, he had managed to hide from me the fact that he was involved with another woman, as in seeing her every day he wasn't seeing me. When I found out, I said, "Totally cool. I don't do liars. I've said that from Day One, so you go your way, I'll go mine." He begged and begged me to come back, went to therapy, blamed it on his abusive childhood, and swore he would never lie again. Guess how many times over the past nineteen years I caught him in lies? And he never, ever came to me with the truth. I had to catch him red-handed, so who knows how many I don't even know about.

4. "Know your worth." We all deserve to have a partner who adores us, cherishes us, tells us the truth no matter what, is loyal, has integrity, and makes us laugh our asses off.

5. "Don't lower your standards."

Chapter 33
Get Up, Carry On, Don't be Smashed: Thoughts on Holidays during a Global Pandemic

Divorce and death seem especially piercing during holidays. I don't know why.

Certainly global pandemics and worldwide quarantines don't help matters. In fact, they do quite a bit of piercing themselves.

It's something to ponder while I sit here on this rainy morning, drinking my cappuccino with its whipped foam. I'm surrounded by pink peeps, Cadbury eggs, and dyed Easter Eggs, which of course makes me think of new life, babies, and things piercing their own way out of the cold hard earth of winter.

It also makes me think of how my marriage was a lot like a peep: it looked pretty on the outside but the inside was a sticky toxic gooey mess. Which I suppose I need to remember when I'm feeling forlorn, that no amount of pink sugar can cover up the poison that comes with a marriage built on lies.

Sigh.

At least my cappuccino is divine—every sip feels like falling in love.

I try to focus on the magic of the kids and me, the three of us and I try not to think that one of us is missing.

I have heard that a triangle, a polygon with three edges and vertices, is the most stable physical shape and so is widely used in construction and engineering.

I like that. I'm going to think of the three of us as the most stable structure.

Also, in many cultures, three is a sacred number. The moon goes dark for three days, and in the Christian Easter tradition, it was three days after Christ was killed that he came back to life. It is the holy trinity, the triple goddess, the trimurti (Hinduism) and triple Bodhi (Buddhism). Good and bad things come in threes, three strikes and you're out, three little pigs, three bears, three coins in the fountain, plant-animal-mineral, three pyramids of Giza, three musketeers and three amigos…

And yet, if I'm completely honest with myself, there were piercing moments during Easter where three little words popped into my head, yelling for my attention. And they weren't "I love you." They were:

I feel lost.

And I don't know how to find my way.

I had a vision of my heart yesterday and it wasn't swirly pink and bursting with rainbows like it should have been. It was battered and forlorn, like an old lighthouse that's seen too many storms. I have various tactics for dealing with the swamp of sadness, and so I put on my earphones and went jogging on the beach by myself in the sunshine. I felt jubilant and joyful, so joyful I ended up being one of those weirdos you see "dance-jogging" down the street to music you can't hear. I love those weirdos. I am one of those weirdos.

Joseph Campbell says that if you can see the path before you clearly, it isn't your path, it's someone else's. Your own path you make with every step. Maybe that's why I feel lost.

Anyway, I came home from my dance-jog and my teenagers were eating breakfast. I pulled out the book I gave my daughter last week for her 16th birthday. It's an extraordinary book, very simple, short, profound and beautiful. It's called *The Boy, the Mole, the Fox and the Horse* by Charlie Mackesy.

When my children were little, I spent most of their mealtimes and bedtimes reading to them. It's been a while since

I read to them while they ate, but I plunged in over the protests of my 16-year-old daughter, and as soon as I started they both were instantly quiet, just like when they were little. In it, the boy echoes my own feelings.

"Sometimes I feel lost," said the boy.

"Me too." Said the mole, "but we love you, and love brings you home."

"What is the bravest thing you've ever said?" asked the boy.

"Help," said the horse...

"When have you been at your strongest?" asked the boy.

"When I dared to show my weakness. Asking for help isn't giving up," said the horse. "It's refusing to give up."

"When big things feel out of control... focus on what you love right under your nose."

I think most of us can agree that big things feel out of control right now.

"Don't measure how valuable you are by the way you are treated."

It was after reading this line that I unexpectedly burst into tears. My kids jumped off their barstools and ran around the counter to hug me as I cried.

"Tears fall for a reason and they are your strength, not weakness."

If tears are strength, then I am the freaking Rock. (Sidenote, I had a dream about The Rock last night.)

My 13- year-old son, Henry said, "I don't think this book is for kids. This book is REALLY deep."

Which made us all laugh.

Then Henry said, "If I was a character in this book, I'd be the mole because I love cake." There's a wise mole character in the book, who keeps trying to bring cake to his friends, but eats the cakes before he can gift them.

Every sentence in the book is amazing, but the next line, seemed really important for the kids to hear, although now I think maybe the person who needed to hear it the most was me.

"Always remember you matter, you're important and you are loved, and you bring to this world things no one else can."

Every single person brings things to the world that no one else can. Walked in your shoes. Only me, was raised in a Mormon community by Mexican witches, moved to Hollywood and lived with my soulmate and best friend, danced onstage for years for thousands of people, worked with terminally ill children, traveled around the world with no money and landed at Harvard at the age of 32, leading me to marriage and magical children, and what I thought was my fairy tale, only to have my marriage implode and my soulmate/best friend decide to leave the planet early…

And here I am, a single mom who needs to find a job during a global pandemic, who has been home with my children for the last sixteen years and who's previous work experience includes circus acrobatics, belly dancing and go-go dancing, leaving me with absolutely no idea what kind of job I might be qualified for… unless someone wants to pay me for my current talent of rolling off my very deep and delicious Lovesac couch—which requires more strength and flexibility than you might think. And I'm getting Olympic level practice at this skill during this quarantine.

And there is one more very important reminder in the book:

"Sometimes just getting up and carrying on is brave and magnificent."

Hemingway said the same thing with different words:

"The first and final thing you have to do in this world is to last it and not be smashed by it."

So there you go, two things to focus on during holidays: get up and carry on… and don't be smashed by the world.

Chapter 34
Running Barefoot Through the Apple Orchard

My friend Courtney is always encouraging me to start dating, making me online profiles, offering to start small fires at my house when she visits from Alaska, so we can call the firefighters.

(She knows how much I love a hunky firefighter–I mean come on, those muscles, that devotion to caring for people– and if anyone needs to be carried out of a burning building right now, it's me.)

I feel like my whole life has become a burning building lately and I could really use a little help fighting the fires, so I can get the hell out.

Yes please

In any case, I have always loved romance and courtship. I love a gentleman bringing me gifts, laughing at my jokes, eating my cookies… I adore a generous soul, a caretaker, and someone who loves sparkles and twinkling lights like I do. So when I ran into a certain guy at the store the other night on a late night shopping spree with my friend, Cristie, I texted Courtney and said, "Guess what? I've been meaning to tell you I met someone. He's wonderful–husky, kind, generous, loves cookies and twinkle lights."

She replied, "No way!! Who is he??"

I said, "Nick." And sent a photo of me and the adorable little Santa I stumbled upon at the grocery store. I walked by Santa, he caught my eye, and I decided he was perfect for me. I couldn't stop laughing at myself, but Courtney wasn't amused.

She texted me back an emoji of rolling eyes. Or *maybe* she was amused–there's a reason she's one of my best friends–we make each other laugh until we are rolling on the floor holding our stomachs. I met her thirty years ago when we were both working graveyard shifts at Canters Bakery in Hollywood. She was working to pay off debt, I was working five jobs to save money for a semester in Paris. I was paid $5.11 per hour. She was only one year older than me, but she seemed so wise back then.

She keeps telling me to get out there, and I keep saying no, I'm not ready. How can I possibly go out with someone when my life is in shambles? What would I say? "Hi, my life is a burning building. I am drowning in grief. How are you?" It seems impossible. What if they are awful? Liars? Bad breath? Dandruff? Like my ex? Yuck! No thank you.

Then Courtney sent me this quote by Louise Erdich.

"Life will break you. Nobody can protect you from that, and living alone won't either, for solitude will also break you with its yearning. You have to love. You have to feel. It is the reason you are here on earth. You are here to risk your heart. You are here to be swallowed up. And when it happens that you are broken, or betrayed, or left, or hurt, or death brushes near, let yourself sit by an apple tree and listen to the apples falling all around you in heaps, wasting their sweetness. Tell yourself you tasted as many as you could."

Well said, Ms. Erdich. I love an apple orchard and I always have.

I grew up running barefoot through Mr. Farley's apple orchard. I can still see the red apples, my ten-year-old hand twisting and tugging until they came off the tree, the red skin warm from the sun, and that first juicy crunch, the sweet liquid dripping down my chin. I can still smell the trees, the fallen apples rotting back into the earth, the branches rough to the touch, and perfect for climbing.

The branches slope in a way that cradles you, so you can lie comfortably for hours in an apple tree. I still remember the stillness and quiet of the orchard as I cut through it on my way home, the grass up to my knees, the sun beating on my head, my hands and chin sticky with apple juice, the only sound was my footsteps. And occasionally, a pheasant would startle me, lifting off the ground right in front of me in a flurry of wings, making my heart jump so high it would take several minutes to get it back to it's normal pace.

I suppose those surprise pheasants were good training for life, because really, I was just walking along through my 40's, marveling at the beauty of life when:

"SURPRISE! Flurry Flutter!" Your father's gone!

"SURPRISE! Bam!" Your husband's gone!

"SURPRISE! Thwack Smack Crush! Your best friend's gone!

I'm still trying to get my heartbeat back to normal.

But you know what helps?

Apple orchards.

And even now when I feel like I will never love again, I call my friend Jacquie and say, "Are you SURE that life will get better? Are you POSITIVE that other doors will open?" She replies, "I'm 100% positive." And I want to believe her. She has faith for both of us when mine is MIA.

Here in New England, I go to the apple orchards in the summer, take off my shoes and climb the strongest-looking tree barefoot, just like I did as a child. I sit on a branch, quietly breathing, just letting the tree branches support me. I know I look cuckoo–the crazy lady who sits barefoot in the apple trees — but I don't care. It's important.

And I think about my Dad. He loved apple orchards. Some of my favorite memories of him involve lying on the grass under a tree in our backyard, eating apples and looking at the sky.

Then I think about my daughter. When she was five months old, I wanted to honor her first food and her first steps away from me. I took her to an apple orchard and helped her tiny chubby fingers pick an apple. I made her a batch of applesauce, telling her I hoped the same sunshine, wind, and rain that grew those apples would nourish her soul and body, so she could grow strong enough to withstand any storm. She was a baby and didn't understand a word I said, but I hoped it floated around her like a fairy wish and would sink in somewhere, making magic for her. Then I gave her a bite and she made a face like it was the most disgusting thing she had ever tasted. The applesauce was bitter–I should have added sugar to sweeten it for her.

But I suppose it's an important lesson that sometimes beautiful things taste bitter, and sometimes they taste sweet. And maybe that's what I need to do as I move on from my marriage: acknowledge that sometimes the apples might be bitter, and sometimes they will be sweet, but the only way to know is to start tasting.

As long as I'm not sitting next to my little sister. We were on a road trip when we were little, and I was sitting next to her eating an apple and looking out the window, feeling the warm mountain air on my face, when she suddenly grabbed the apple out of my hand mid-bite and threw it out the window. Literally. I was left with my hand in the air and my mouth open. What the heck?

I don't know, but I do know a good place to think about the philosophical constructs of apples, is in the little farmhouse at the orchard. I love to go in late Autumn near sunset and sit on the wooden rocking chair in front of the roaring fire, with a cup of hot cider in one hand and a hot cider donut in the other. I rock in the creaky chair and think, wrapped in my faux fur, feeling cozy and warm inside and out. And I think, maybe I don't need to *find* a firefighter, maybe I need to *be* a firefighter myself.

As my daughter, now fifteen, reminds me every day, "MOM! YOU ARE the hero!" And she's right – I rescue the kids all day every day, and will forever. But I can't do any rescuing of anyone unless I am standing tall and strong myself.

The only way I can start tasting apples is knowing my sisters, and Courtney, and the rest of my amazing tribe are nearby so I can share every part of my experiences, the good and the bad. Even if they occasionally rip an apple out of my hand and toss it out the window. I know they will boo the bad and cheer the good, and that gives me a little more courage to maybe get out there.

But not right now. Right now, I sit in front of the huge crackling fire, my cheeks red from the heat, and imagine myself not *fighting* the fire, but *enjoying* its wild heat. I dip my donut in my cider, tasting the hot melting apple in my mouth and ponder.

Chapter 35
Sisters

Late last night, I was standing in the kitchen wearing my pink flannel champagne pajamas, when my teenagers came home from a party hosted by a theater friend, who has recently become a self-proclaimed witch. They told me how mid-party he brought out a crystal ball and fell into a psychic trance where his eyes rolled back in his head. He told them to follow their dreams.

Their description was interrupted by my older sister, Maria, who is visiting for the holiday. She came jumping into the room like she had an invisible jumprope, wearing pink pajamas that matched mine.

She hopped around the dining room table chanting a "jumprope song" from our childhood:
"Crystal Ball!
Please tell me!
What kind of man will marry me?
Rich man? Poor man? Beggar man? Thief?
Doctor? Lawyer? Indian chief?"

She chanted at the top of her lungs while hopping around, as we all burst out laughing, except my teen son who was lying on the couch making a Tik Tok on his iPad and wouldn't look up. She hopped over to him and sat on him, chanting and waving her arms till he was laughing so hard he could barely sit up.

I haven't heard that song since I was probably 8 years old, and vague cotton candy memories floated back to me while she chanted; memories of bare feet on the hot street, skinned knees, callused hands rubbed by the rope, chalk on the ground from hopscotch…

I have told my children many times that my greatest wish for them is that they have each other the way I have my sisters, Marlise and Maria. Growing up in the same house together, we have a shorthand language that no one else knows.

(For example, we know that Maria had the hots for Neal Diamond and saw the Jazz Singer 34 times in the theater. We know that Marlise took scissors to my childhood poster of Andy Gibb because she didn't like his hairy chest. We know every boy Maria dated because Marlise and I used to spy on her through the venetian blinds in our room as she said goodnight to her dates on the porch, to see if she kissed anyone.)

Maria worked at The Limited at our local mall and ended up managing it at the age of 16. She ended up marrying her college football player beau, having three sons, now has a million grandkids. A fiery no-nonsense Virgo with a very bossy nature, Maria has usually ended up running every company she works for, and would make a great CEO.

Then there's my little sister, Marlise. She is the picture of compassion and kindness. We always shared a room growing up and were so close our parents used to tell us we would have conversations while sleeping. She has six kids—yes you heard right, six! She married her high school sweetheart, had four children, then adopted two more from Haiti. She is now a teacher at her kid's high school. We all are really busy, pulled in many different directions: Kids! Work! Marriage! Divorce! But we talk on the phone every day and make time to see each other as often as possible.

The last two years of my life have been a total flooding of tragedy, like the smashing destruction and achingly slow sinking of the Titanic, my sisters have been my lifeboat. They have both flown in several times, and most recently, Maria came for the holiday. I didn't even know how badly I needed her physical presence until I burst into tears when we hugged at the airport.

Both of them flew in when our father was in his last days. We had trouble managing his pain and my little sister rode in the ambulance with him to hospice while Maria and I followed in my car. My brothers flew in and we all stayed by my Dad's side all day, taking turns staying with him at night.

When my sisters ended up coming home with me, they dragged me out to walk to the beach two blocks from my house. We walked out on the sand, the three of us, and talked, and cried, and laughed, and pretended to hold the moon in our hands.

(It wasn't all moonlight and hand-holding. There are agonizing memories that I push away when they flood my mind: things like black vomit, my Dad bunching up his blanket over and over again in his beautiful once-strong hands while murmuring things we couldn't hear, everyone running in circles as our great and fearless leader shrunk and shriveled before our eyes. They wouldn't let us give him food or water, and it was unbearable to watch him suffer.)

Kim flew in to help me with the kids so I could be with my Dad. She brought them to the hospice so they could say goodbye, and my Dad always loved Kim. She asked us if we wanted her to sing for my Dad. We all nodded yes. There was something about the vibrations of live music that sets up a net of some sort around all of us in the room with my Dad. It was comforting in a way that goes beyond time and space. Kim had a beautiful singing voice. She sang a gorgeous soft version of "Somewhere Over the Rainbow" for my Dad, her hand resting lightly on the blanket over his feet, a huge smile on her face as she sang to him, to me, to all of us. Then she took the kids home and made cookies with them and played games.

But all of us, my Mom and us kids, stayed by my Dad's side, talking, singing, dancing, laughing, doing pushups (my brother) and occasionally arguing. Then we'd take a walk outside in the gardens of the hospice, before returning to the sacred space of watching over my Dad. Near the end, Maria got mad at me about something (I don't remember what) and decided to return home. I said, "What? I thought you said you were staying till the end!" She stood there, chomping her gum with her cop sunglasses on, tears streaming down her face, "No, you got this."

"Hold on, are you mad about something? Because at this point I hope you know better than to ever take offense to anything I say. I don't even know what I'm saying half the time. I'm overwhelmed, very overwhelmed, and if I say something you don't like, just tell me to shut the hell up, but don't leave."

She nodded, changed her flight to stay, and was standing next to me holding my Dad as he took his last breath.

I can't even tell you the searing loss for all of us of such a soul.

He was an extraordinary father because he was funny as hell, but also a pillar of integrity and loyalty. He loved and prioritized us over work, wealth, and accomplishment, but never had to *tell* us because he *showed* us through his actions and his life choices over and over again.

At the last breath, my Mom was confused, arguing with the nurse, fussing over my Dad, straightening the sheet, kissing his head over and over again until Maria and I took her in our arms, so strangers could carry away her great love.

She never recovered from losing him, and we haven't either. And having my sisters to grieve with lightens the heaviness a little We can call each other crying, and we don't need any explanation because we know.

Even in their own grief, my sisters have been with me as I was hit over and over with Titanic-level crashes.

They were irate when they learned how my ex-husband had betrayed me, and heartbroken when I called them to tell them about Kim. Maria sent me a pink tree. Marlise sent me wind chimes engraved with Kim's name and said, "We grieve with you."

Every time I walk by the wind chimes, I tap them so their beautiful sound will wash over me and I'll imagine Kim is here with me, and my sisters.

So on Maria's last day here, her plane got delayed and the kids had a glorious snow day. We all decided to watch *Stranger Things*.

We love snow days at our house: slippers, hot cocoa, roaring fires, snow angels, snow ice cream, and movie marathons.

But on this snow day, I was having a hard time staying present with the kids because my phone was ringing off the hook with divorce drama. Some very dark people were seriously yucking my yum by screaming vitriol in my ear and making me aware of devious duplicitous dealings.

At this age, I shouldn't be surprised by nasty people, but I always am.

And as I watched *Stranger Things*, I realized, the trauma of divorce is like the Upside Down. I look around and it looks like my house, my neighborhood, my yard, but it's dark and cold and toxic, and there are faceless monsters waiting to pounce, slimy slithering darkness aggressively coming after you, trying to destroy all that's beautiful and positive, leaving your world cold, empty, dark.

The air in the Upside Down is so toxic, it's hard to breathe.
The air in the Divorce Drama World is so toxic, it's hard to breathe.

My sister took charge. (I told you she was bossy.) She answered calls, conference-called my other sister, and discussed ways to deal with the Demogorgons.

I sat next to my sister in the greenhouse with the flowers blooming, the waterfalls flowing, the twinkle lights twinkling, and listened and chimed in. But finally, I dealt with it the only way I knew how.

I turned my phone off and ran out into the snow. The branches heavy and curving with whipped cream sparkles, the dogs leaping with every step, my beloved teenagers sitting in the snow with a bottle of maple syrup, making snow ice cream, looking like they did as toddlers. It was such a magical moment, as I stood in knee-high snow and reveled: the two of them together, laughing and talking and tasting snow.

And I keep telling them, my greatest wish for them is that they have each other the way I have my sisters.

My sisters know me better than anyone because we know each other's hearts. We cheer each other on, believe the best in each other always, and rush to any one of us who needs help. We can talk for years about important world issues like losing ten pounds, cutting bangs, shopping mania, and we are also first responders to each other, when one of us calls sobbing. I can say whatever crazy thing enters my mind, and my sisters will fall on the floor laughing, and then say something to make me fall on the floor laughing.

On the Titanic, they would throw the lifeboat right to me.

In the Upside Down, they will put on their Hazmat suits and march into save me every time.

And if I had a crystal ball, I think it would tell me to stay in my yummy world, that light and love, the laughter of my sisters and my kids, my own clear heart, will blast out the yuck every time.

Chapter 36
Can a Pair of Purple Velvet Boots With Upturned Toes Turn Pain into Humor? I say YES! (It's Worth a Try, Right?)

To overcome the slings and arrows of life, (and when I say slings and arrows, I mean slings and arrows with nuclear bombs attached to them because dealing with the trauma of death and divorce often feels like complete annihilation,) I recommend finding humor and if you can't find it, make it. Woo! I'm breathless from that awesome run-on sentence! Find humor every day, and if you can't find it, create it.

Here is the list I have written on my bathroom mirror:
Make mischief.
Be cheeky.
Buy a pair of purple velvet shoes with upturned toes.
Work in a wand shop that smells of whiskey and absinthe.
Prance like a unicorn... But I'm getting ahead of myself.

I try to find humor and make mischief every day, most obviously in the way I dress, and I've found that the more pain I'm in, the more colorful I dress. It's almost like magical thinking: if I'm wearing bright colors and sparkling boots, I will feel bright and sparkling. Weirdly, it often works.

I've always had a unique sense of style. I remember in high school that I never liked to wear the same thing twice. My personal style theme was "wildly romantic" and I would look at Betsey Johnson in Vogue or watch a Marilyn Monroe movie, and I would model an outfit based on that inspiration. After watching *Mary Poppins*, I remember going into my mother's closet, pulling out a red floral "moo-moo," which is what she called her loose-fitting dresses worn on Sundays after church, so she could eat as much as she wanted for Sunday dinners and not worry about loosening her belt. I put on the "moo-moo" and tied up the back with a ribbon to make a bustle, similar to the Edwardian dresses worn by Julie Andrews in *Mary Poppins*, and I wore it to school. A while later, my fashionista sister, Marlina, bought a Norma Kamali dress made of brocade that was shaped like a Mary Poppins Edwardian-style dress I strived to create. I begged to borrow the dress and wore it to church with a big hat and a long veil over my face. I was fifteen.

My parents found me very entertaining and to their credit, never tried to squelch my creative expression. I would climb into the car in my outrageous outfits, and they would just keep talking like nothing unusual had just entered the car. Other people would burst into laughter when they saw me, and I would hold my head high and swagger by, ignoring their guffaws. Incredibly, I was never deterred by these reactions, and in fact, didn't really care what people thought. If I liked the outfit and it made me feel good, I wore it. Judgers be damned! All these years later, I'm still dressing crazy and still evoking laughter, which I like to think of as delight in my whimsy, but is probably closer to plain old laughter at some crazy sartorial ensembles.

So, a few years ago, I went to Witch-a-Palooza at Gardner Village in Utah, an enchanting celebration of witches. I wandered into a shop and my heart sang when I spotted a pair of purple velvet witch shoes, with a curving turned up toe, so I tried them on. My one rule for shoes is they must make me strut, leap, swagger and hop. If they cause that much delight, then I bring them home. I didn't have plans for when or where to wear them, but sometimes I buy things as "Closet Candy," meaning they make my closet even more delightful with their presence, whether or not I ever wear them.

The purple witch shoes–I made a place to wear them!

Fast forward to the day my daughter dragged me into Forever 21. "No!" I protested as she pulled me inside. "I hate these crap stores with their piles of junky clothes. I can't find anything and it's overwhelming and makes me dizzy.... What's that?" I ran over to a rack of fluffy faux fur in icy baby blue. I found a Size Large and put it on, ranning to the mirror. "OMG! It's GORGEOUS!! What do you think?"

"I love it," Annabelle laughed with an eye-roll, as she picked up my purse that I had dropped in my excitement.

I checked the price tag. $20.00. I looked up at the walls, the ceiling and said in a voice of wonder, "What is this place?" I ran from rack to rack, and in the end, I came home with three new faux fur coats in stunning colors. I called the coats "chubbies" because of their length. When I show up anywhere and someone is cold, I say, "Would you like to borrow my chubby?" (This brings no end to the hilarity of my friends who have a different meaning for the word "chubby.")

To me, a "chubby" is a glamorous 1950's style waist-length coat, perfect for autumn nights at the opera or spring trips in carpool.

WHAT?? I created a place to wear my witch shoes AND the furry coat!! YES!!

Which brings me to yesterday at the Wand Shop. I live next to Salem, home of witch-mania and all sorts of magical shops and people. When my son turned 6, I threw him a Harry Potter birthday party at the haunted (for real!) Hawthorne Hotel, and I found a shop next to the hotel that sold incredible wands and all manner of jaw-dropping Harry Potter stuff.

Flash forward a few more years, and I decided it would be fun to work in the Wand Shop as holiday help during Halloween. Thousands of extra people descend into Salem during October, and there is no end to the incredible people-watching. I coerced my festive and hilarious Martini Club member, Cristie Carter, to join me in applying to the job. Cristie is one of the funniest people I know and she's always up for an adventure. I call her the "Cristie Vortex" because I'll meet her for coffee and seven hours later we are driving down the freeway with pumpkin lattes in hand, feathered witch hats on our heads and a Suburban full of shopping bags, singing *Truth Hurts* by Lizzo as loud as we can, and dancing car-hip-hop as only middle-aged moms can. Cristie is the person you want to sit next to at any boring school event–she will have you on the floor laughing. She finds humor in every tiny thing, and I'm always fascinated by the way her mind works. For example, once our girls were in our living room at Halloween time, lamenting the fact that they were headed to a school dance, but weren't sure how to dance a slow dance. Cristie promptly grabbed two life size skeletons I had set up as Halloween props and did a demonstration with them of how to dance, turning an awkward moment for our budding teens into a hilarious moment.

We went together to the Wand Shop to apply. The owner knows me so we didn't *really* apply, we showed up and offered to help him out during the high Salem holiday. Then we went to have margaritas on the roof to celebrate our new jobs. It was a sunny Autumn day and the roof of the Salem Hotel offers fabulous views of the harbor and pirate schooners. On the way back to our cars, we popped into my favorite shop, Modern Millie, and $500 later, with shopping bags full of purses in the shape of movie popcorn, pink glittering dinosaurs and dresses covered in frolicking cats, we left for carpool. Mind you, it would take us three months of working full time to pay off the ten-minute shopping spree.

In any case, the wand shop is the opposite of Forever 21.

First of all, it smells like the Whiskey and Absinthe scented candles, which they have burning in every corner. It is all dark wood, and the soaring magical music from Potter swoops around the shop at all times, making you feel like you are in an enchanting movie.

The owner is a talented set decorator. He has filled the upper parts of the shop with old rolls from player pianos stacked all over like scrolls, and their boxes, which are the exact same size as wands, stacked everywhere. The heater flickers like a fireplace. There are witch brooms everywhere, some with magical creatures carved into the sticks. Antique-looking leather spell books line the shelves, feather quills, and wands of every type are on display everywhere—elderwood, bloodwood, walnut, gnarled oak. Some are carved in a spiral, some are pink for cheering spells, and some have jewels encrusted into the handles. They are all different lengths with beautiful handles, and shaped in different ways to evoke different energy. One style wand is shaped like a violin to bring harmony into your home, while another has points on each end so whatever spell you cast out will cast on you too.

The people-watching is priceless. Yesterday a man came into the shop, dressed in head-to-toe pirate style. "A pirate costume!" I cooed. The man, who was probably around sixty, said, "Not a costume. More a way of life." Then he said, "Arrrgghhh" and bought a Butterbeer. I told you, priceless.

Covens of real-practicing witches ages 5-75 come in together wearing sparkling witch hats. One woman comes in wearing sunglasses and shyly lays a book about love spells on the counter. Children dressed like vampires, witches, princesses run through the shop and buy pink wands or delicate seashell wands. A mother buys her teenage daughter and her friend matching wands and matching purple cloaks. People come from all over the world, showing me their tattoos of the triangle, circle and wand with the word *Always* next to it, buying Slytherin patches, Gryffindor robes, Tarot cards, asking us how to read them. (I don't know.) There two canaries in the window named Fred and George that tweet and hop around in their cage, while customers tap the cage and coo at them.

In addition to Cristie, who runs around putting owls on her head and showing people how to use a time-travel piece, I work with Rose Wolf, a self-ordained professor and high-ranking witch in Salem. She teaches workshops on the poetry of Emily Dickinson and is in some sort of epic falling out with the highest ranked witch in Salem, Laurie Cabot. I don't know the details, but I do love watching the drama unfold. With her short spiky black hair, eyes rimmed with thick black liner, and heavy silver rings on her fingers, Rose looks like she answered a casting call for a vintage Metallica music video. She dusts and cleans the shop nonstop, picking up an old clock and dusting it before the face falls off completely. After a few tries of getting it back on, she sticks it in the back of the shop with a laugh for future repair. She mutters to herself while she cleans the shop between customers, and this time of year, there are so many wanting to come into the shop, they have to put up a rope and a bouncer to organize the lines. But sometimes it's not so crazy, and when the bell jangles, signaling that a customer has entered, she talks to them while she cleans. She has a collection of wand jokes and puns that she slips into nearly every conversation. "I'm guessing you are here because you "wand' a wand? Remember you don't choose a wand, the wand chooses you! Isn't that a gorgeous wood? Made right here at the shop by our Master Wandmaker, Joe. He's the only one in the country who can carve a piece of elderwood into a perfect spiral like that. He's also a Master Warlock and blesses each wand with his magic. The elderwood protects you from misfortune and helps you to banish and recreate a new reality. What are you looking for? Well it does that too. Now if you're looking for a different wand, this wand is a cheering wand. It's pink, which is proven to lift moods. They are now painting prisons that color. And of course it emulates the unicorn horn, the unicorn, the symbol of purity, innocence, truth, faithfulness. Even in medieval times when they wove a unicorn into their tapestry and painted them on their cathedral walls. That wand is a special kind of magic because it resembles the horn of the precious and faithful unicorn."

While she talks, I imagine myself as a unicorn prancing among the rainbows!! Or maybe I'm a bubbling cauldron of burning bones, whiskey, and absinthe trying her darnedest to not overflow and disappear in a puff of smoke.

A few hours in the wand shop with Rose Wolf and Cristie, a furry coat, and a pair of velvet shoes with upturned toes make it all easier to bear.

And I will leave you with this little joke I wrote to amuse myself as I try my darnedest to turn the pain of divorce into humor. Those who know my ex are not surprised by the turn of events that caused the divorce. They say, "Marci, a spade is always a spade." To which I reply, "Unless that spade is disguised as a ho, which he was." Be-dum-dum.

Chapter 37
Malarkey! Poppycock! Balderdash! Horsefeathers!

What are these fabulous words, you ask?

Well, yes, they are fabulous 1920's slang, but for me, they are light-hearted synonyms for the world of divorce.

Although if any of you have ever gone through a divorce, you know there's nothing light-hearted about it. In fact, it's quite heavy-hearted, akin to the feeling of dropping your heart into a cauldron of fire while the shysters slither around throwing mazuma on the flames to make them burn brighter.

Of course, these words aren't in common use today, but as someone who thinks 1920's slang is the cats pajamas, I'd like to bring them back. They are far more fun to say than, "I call bullshit!" which is just a little too… base and vivid as far as imagery goes.

So, Divorce World is full of so much blather and bunkum I could write an entire book about it, and as luck would have it, that's exactly what I have done! So here I thought I'd share a bit of the tomfoolery, trash, and twaddle that comes with divorce.

There's one specific phrase that keeps being said in Divorce World that needs its own special shelf in the trophy cabinet of divorce hooey and it is this:

"I'm a better father (or in some cases, mother) now that I'm out of the home than I was in the home."

Or

"I couldn't be the father I wanted to be while in the house, so I had to leave to become a better dad."

Hmmmmm. Some people might call that an absentee father, a toxic father, a selfish narcissistic father...

It's kind of like saying, "I lit my children's hair on fire, but I'm a better father for it!"

Or, "I stomped on the heart of my children's mother while they watched, then I stomped on their hearts too, but I'm a better father for it, so ... yeah for me!"

Right. A phrase like this calls for the old Bronx Cheer. (That means blowing a raspberry to show your disapproval, which you may feel free to do throughout this essay.)

It sounds a lot like someone trying to make themselves feel better after shattering their family.

I come from a different world, where creating a family is considered an honor so sacred that we hold big rituals where we vow in front of the world and everything we hold dear to love, cherish, and protect each other for time and all eternity. It's called a *wedding*. In this magical world, people honor their vows and do everything in their power to protect their family from piffle and poppycock, even if it means setting aside their own massive egos and putting their family first.

And if you think creating a family means putting yourself first, *Tell It to Sweeney*.

So here I am, flung into a world of phonus balonus, raising my very own bearcat and dewdropper, and I have to say, it's actually quite ducky, because they are the Bees Knees.
And they make my life Cat's Meow.

So even if the rest of the world just seems to be on a bender, determined to stay zozzled, I'll be here having a riotous hootenanny with my favorite people, my family, and that makes today, in a word or two, Hotsy-Totsy.

1920's Slang that I wish would re-enter the common vernacular (please join me in using these on a regular basis. I promise they make even poppycock fun!)

Malarkey: Nonsense
Poppycock: Nonsense
Horsefeathers: Nonsense
Balderdash: Nonsense
Shyster: Lawyer
Killjoy:
Mazuma: Money
Cat's Pajamas: It's the best!
Blather: Nonsense
Bunkum: Nonsense
Tomfoolery: Nonsense
Trash: Nonsense
Twaddle: Nonsense
Hooey: Nonsense
Tell It to Sweeney: I don't believe you
Phonus Balonus: nonsense
Bearcat: High spirited lively girl
Dewdropper: Someone who likes to sleep all day (this could define pretty much any teenager)
Ducky: great
Bees Knees: It's the best!
Hootenanny: party
Hotsy Totsy: Perfect
Cat's Meow: It's the best!
Bronx Cheer: Blowing a raspberry to signal disapproval

Chapter 38
Moving

So the kids and I just moved. And it's confusing. I walk around our new house sometimes thinking, "Where am I? This doesn't look familiar." And sometimes I feel like I've lived here forever. Often I want to throw everything into storage and sell this house and take off, hit the open road with the kids, listen to amazing music and stories together, have an adventure. And sometimes I vacillate between feeling richer than ever and poorer than a church mouse.

The first thing I wanted to do when my ex jumped ship, was move to be closer to my family, but it didn't seem right to add moving onto the list of stressors for the kids, so we stayed. But the house was our only asset and needed to be sold as part of the divorce. The timing never seemed right, until one day someone messaged me on Facebook with a cash offer and I decided to take it. I called my ex to tell him about the offer, and he said, "Ahh that house is so frustrating! It's so close to being our dream house, but there's always something going wrong with it, and even if we do get back together, I don't think we will want that house."

Seriously, he said that. "Even if we do get back together…"

I didn't respond with what was going through my head, which was the following:

"WTF? Are you on drugs again? Have you lost your ever-loving mind?"

But I didn't say any of it out loud. My ex is volatile and I didn't want to set him off.

He repeated this several times throughout the conversation.

When I hung up, I accepted the offer and we were off to the races. I called a banker friend to walk me through the loan process. It was overwhelming, and there were many many times I wanted to crawl back into bed and pull the covers over my head.

I booked some coaching sessions with Star Monroe, the Queen of Empowering Women. She told me to, "Adult the fuck up." I'm not kidding, she really said that. She said to kick my inner weeping princess to the curb and call on my inner queen. She said the queen could handle all of this and more.

And she was right.

The queen archetype worked for me. I lifted my head and forged on. Every time I wanted to pull the covers over my head, I lifted my head higher and pretended I was a queen overseeing my kingdom.

In addition to packing up our home while supporting and caring for my children, I was tasked with finding somewhere for me and the kids to live. I looked at fifteen houses in two weekends. Some were gorgeous historical mansions like the one we were leaving, and though I always want the beautiful charm, this time I wanted a newer house that didn't require any upkeep, so I could focus on caring for my children and building my writing career.

So I walked into House #16 and the energy felt good.

A great advantage to being divorced is that I don't have to consult with anyone. I said, "I'll take it!"

My ex was very supportive (from a distance) of our move until the morning of the actual move when he decided to pull a fast one. The morning of the move, we were closing on the old house at 8am and closing on the new house at 10 am, so there were a lot of moving parts that required everything to go smoothly.

So as I'm orchestrating the kids, the move, the *everything*, my ex emailed me and the realtors announcing he would not be signing the real estate papers until I changed our divorce agreement.

Seriously.

I was literally standing at my new house *with the moving company* trying to coax him away from Crazyland. He refused to leave Crazyland, unleashing a string of vicious expletives towards me by text. I texted back, "Fine. I will direct the movers back to the old house. We liked that house, we'll just move back in, and you can deal with all the litigation from breaking all the agreements you have made."

Once he realized I wasn't going to dance with the devil, he finally signed, but he insisted on taking the entire deposit from the buyers, refusing to give me my half. Classic douchebag move, and sadly, not surprising. If he can make a situation more stressful for me and the kids, he will.

So we moved in, and I'm still stumbling about wondering where I am? It doesn't feel like it's mine, so to make myself feel better, I dragged all my pink glitter furniture into my living room. Then I unraveled a tattered poster from a cardboard tube and it made me happy to see Audrey Hepburn as Holly Golightly staring back at me, with her big sunglasses and jewels. I have always loved Breakfast at Tiffany's, and in high school drama class, out of all the monologues in the world, I chose to do Holly Golightly during the scene when she's looking for her shoe and getting dressed to go see Sally Tomato. I dragged a ladder over to the garage door and hung the poster over it, so every time we go in and out of the house, Holly Golightly is watching over us like we are jewels.

And isn't that the truth? Home is wherever the three of us are together.

Chapter 39
Lessons I've learned from Holly Golightly:

Big sunglasses and sparkling jewels make everything better.

Some people can eat donuts and never gain weight.

Window-shopping is excellent therapy.

Best to fall asleep naked with full makeup, an eye mask and ear plugs with tassels that look like glamorous earrings.

Keep your phone in a suitcase.

Keep one shoe under your bed and the other on a window, then be sure to look adorable as you crawl around looking for them.

Climbing up and down fire escapes, playing "Moon River" while wearing a kerchief, and eavesdropping on your neighbors is a great form of entertainment.

Every day, do something you have never done before. (Although not shoplifting)

Cats are hard to name. One name is a big commitment, so feel free to change your pet's names as much as you want. (All five of my pets have at least 8 names each.)

Don't marry Buddy Ebsen, he will try to keep you on the farm.

Life is full of lonely damaged people, but that still doesn't mean you should name your cat.

If Holly Golightly is your patron saint, you may want to double-check your life.

Chapter 40
Born Again Virgin

Well, it's been a long time since I've had some lovin'. For someone who loves romance and has a libido on par with a Category 5 hurricane, it feels like 100 years.

But you don't need to feel sorry for me. I'm my own best lover, always have been, so all is not lost.

My sisters and friends say I need to get back out there, start dating, get some action. My friend, Cristie's sister told me it's very important to take a lover right away just to break the spell your ex had over you, to help dispel the rejection and humiliation that goes along with divorce and to know you are sexy and attractive. She says it's like making pancakes, the first few will most likely be really bad, but then they get great.

I do love pancakes, filled with bananas and chocolate chips, smothered in hot maple syrup, but I'm not looking for just any Joe Schmo.

I'm attracted to people's souls, not photos. (Unless they are The Rock or Aquaman, and then the attraction is there regardless of the soul, but it seems they both have amazing souls, so that just increases my attraction.)

But really, I can't imagine dating again. The mere thought of actually going out with someone, explaining to them my life, my heartbreak, who my kids are, who my Dad was, who Kim was, makes me want to throw up.

And I'm very happy by myself, with my kids, with my friends. I'm in Mom mode, not dating mode.

But sometimes I think a little romance might be nice. I used to love to date. Before my last twenty years of marriage, I adored dating. But back then I was out all the time in nightclubs and bars, and meeting lovers was easy. Now my life consists of carpool, homework, and grocery shopping, none of which are hotbeds of love.

I do have gentleman admirers of course. They are lovely, dropping gifts off on my doorstep, meeting me for walks on the beach, asking me out to dinner. My daughter says, "Mom! Go! You are the most romantic person I know! I want you to fall in love!"

She's right, but you can't rush love, right?

I mean, I do have admirers of course, single Dads who invite me out, leave gifts on my porch, walk with me on the beach. And I do adore having admirers, but chemistry can't be made if it isn't there.

If personal ads were still a thing, this would be mine:

If you like pina coladas... (Just kidding)

Passionate, romantic, book-loving artist seeks a sizzling love affair with someone honest, hilarious, loving, cheerful, passionate, and kind. Must love animals, children, books, movies, learning, museums, travel adventures, and sparkles. Looking for someone to frolic with me in the forest (not hike — frolic); drink wine and have all-night discussions on philosophy, art, and beauty; spontaneous slow dances under the moonlight are necessary; and someone who looks at me like starlight is dancing in my hair.

The word 'virgin,' by the way, comes from the same root word as 'virile,' and technically means "strong" or "one unto herself."

There are many cheery perks to being one unto myself.

Number one? I'm a fabulous thoughtful lover and I always smell good.

Two? I don't have to compromise on anything.

Three? I don't have to consult with anyone about buying a house, decorating my house, taking a trip, or buying a pink glitter chair. If I like it, I buy it, plan it, do it. It's liberating and thrilling, to make these decisions on my own. My ex had opposite tastes to me and censored nearly everything I loved. I love incense, velvet, glimmering saris, glitter, feathers, chandeliers — my ex hates all that and when I met him, he said no way was I allowed to put any of my favorite things into our house. That was okay — I loved him more than my velvet, but now I can be surrounded by my favorite things without someone telling me no. I can listen to whatever song I want, light a candle that smells like cookies, and go to bed when I want without someone telling me to do it differently.

Four? When I plan a trip, I get to do exactly what I want. I adore Paris. My ex took me for a weekend in Paris, then announced to me that he hates architecture, museums, history, and basically everything Paris is. Then he worked and was on phone calls for the entire weekend. I took my kids to Paris last summer and I was able to share everything I love about Paris with them: walks on the Seine, museums, art, architecture, swing dancing, amazing food, unexpected adventures...

So, at this exact moment, I'm lying on my pink linen sheets, monogrammed with a big M. My cats are lounging on my feet, and I just finished organizing my fabulous walk-in closets. There are two of them, usually called his and hers, but I call them hers and hers.

So the perks of being a Born Again Virgin are kind of great. Can I get an A-men?

Chapter 41
Busby Berkeley Dreams

Who *doesn't* adore Busby Berkeley? Those innovative camera angles, twirling feathers, whirling stages, and hundreds of stunning showgirls creating a fantasy world of frothy pink carousels, blooming flowers, rushing waterfalls, and glittering snowflakes. I can spot a Busby Berkeley number anywhere, and they light me up deep in my soul with their sheer awesome beauty. They are sublime in the truest meaning of the word, meaning you stand there unable to speak because you are looking at something so beautiful it goes beyond words.

And that's how I felt about my marriage.

In my mind, my groom was wearing a tuxedo and a top hat, and I was wearing a sparkling gown trimmed in feathers that swirled into a sea of sparkles with every twirl, and we were dancing through an outrageously beautiful life together. It's apropos that "our song" was *Busby Berkeley Dreams* by Magnetic Fields.

It encapsulates so much of our relationship.

I should have forgotten you long ago, but you're in every song I know..."

I met my ex in 1999 at a record release party at the Viper Room in LA. I had decided 1999 was the year I would make all my dreams come true, just in case Y2K wiped us all off the face of the planet. So two weeks into 1999, I met my ex. He was the president of some record label and had produced an album for my dear friend, Chuck E. Weiss. Chuck E. had written a song on the album for me called "Oh Marci." It was a kind of pirate French gibberish song, and Chuck E. said he had put a code word in it so my friend would know it was my song. The code word was "Coco," the name of my cat. Chuck E. loves cats, and he had given me a kitten as a gift. I named the gift Coco Bojangles. So here I was at Chuck E.'s record release party in my black lace sparkling gown, dancing and dreaming as usual.

My ex always told me that when he saw me, it was like a bolt of lightning and he had never seen such a beautiful face. I also felt the lightning blast through me when I saw him. He was my type: nerdy, tall, messy hair, glasses. But he lived in a far away land called Massachusetts and I planned to stay in LA forever, so that night at The Viper became just a beautiful memory. We would both ask Chuck E. about each other, but that was the extent of our relationship, until two years later when I decided to go to grad school at Harvard. My ex was the only person I had ever met from MA so I asked Chuck E. for the number of "that guy from the Viper Room two years ago," so I would know at least one person.

We had a Busby Berkeley courtship. I'm talking whirling stages, glittering veils, hot buttered rum candles and a connection so strong the world erupted into a cloud of starlight when we were together. I was getting my Masters degree and my mind was getting blown daily... and being courted by my ex, my heart was getting blown nightly. He swept me off my feet with incredible meals, vibrant discussions, nighttime walks to the lighthouse, homemade molten lava chocolate cake, stunning flowers, heaps of gifts, diamonds from Tiffany's, ski trips, and of course, music. He wrote me many, many love songs, like "As Long as My Baby's Near" and "You Brighten the Corners," which he sang to me at our wedding. "All the nights and all the days, I dreamt of you/waking up, only to find grayness around it all/ and you, you brighten the corners."

I was head over heels for him, well, as it turns out, part of him, my fantasy part, the Busby Berkeley part.

Growing up, the biggest lesson my father ingrained in me was this: "Be honest and let the cards fall where they may." Lying is/was/will always be a deal breaker for me. I told my ex that many times, as he held me and said how lucky for us that we were both such sticklers for honesty, then proceeded to spend the next twenty years spinning an epic web of lies so wide and intricate I could no longer tell what was up and what was down.

Whining and pining is wrong and so on and so forth
Of course, of course,
But no, you can't have a divorce
I haven't seen you in ages, but it's not as bleak as it seems
We still dance on whirling stages in my Busby Berkeley Dreams.

When I caught him in epic lies, which I did a few times over the years, he waged a love bombing campaign so massive I was pulled back in. There were more diamonds from Tiffany's, and pink sand beaches rented for just the two of us, moonlit dinners in remote jungles, Paris trips, sobbing on his knees and begging me to stay, more beautiful songs written for me and recorded while weeping, going to therapy and saying he had worked out his issues and he'd never lie again.

Every time, I was still whirling on our Busby Berkeley stage, so I'd reach out my hand and say yes, let's try again. I wanted to whirl with him forever.

The tears have stained all the pages of my true romance magazine

I was crushed when my marriage ended. But how could I live with myself if I chose to stay with someone who couldn't tell the truth? What example would that set for my children? That it was okay to allow themselves to be treated like a doormat? That is was okay to stay in a relationship full of the bone-burning sizzling sting of betrayal over and over again? Now, when I feel despair and the dark trenches of sadness, I ask myself is there a person in the world who will never betray me? And I can look in the mirror and see that one person in the world who will never betray me. It is me. *I will never betray me again.*

Last week he sent me a selfie, which he does on occasion, and sometimes I see his face and I'm overwhelmed with love for that face I know so well. I have gazed on that face in the golden glow of love on the pillow next to me for almost two decades. It was the face that pressed against mine for life's most sacred and intimate moments: holding my hand when I gave birth to our children; on his knees mopping up the blood when we lost a joyful pregnancy; reaching back to take my hand when we evacuated from New Orleans and I was sitting in back with the baby. It was his hands that lifted my father out of the bathtub when he could no longer stand on his own.

Sigh.

But sometimes with those selfies, my ex doesn't even look familiar—he looks scary and dangerous, and I think, "I wouldn't want to meet this person in a dark alley. I would run towards the light to get myself to safety."

Which is exactly what I did.

Now, I still lie in my pink puffy bed in the dark of night, and I place one hand over my broken heart, and close my eyes, feeling myself dancing on a whirling stage. Sometimes my ex is with me in his tux and top hat, and hot tears run down my cheeks, pooling in my ears. But other times, the best times, it's just me on that stage, with my two beautiful children; one wearing his own tux and top hat, and the other in her own swirling magnificent gown made of starlight and fire. Every time we all twirl, my gown spins out into sparkling golden blossoms of truth that rain down over the three of us.

I haven't seen you in ages
But it's not as bleak as it seems
We still dance on whirling stages
In my Busby Berkeley dreams.

Chapter 42
The Book of Longings: Declaring Your Deepest Dreams to the World in Golden Ink on an Incantation Bowl

I just finished reading Sue Monk Kidd's new novel, *The Book of Longings,* and there were so many parts that struck and inspired me. Her writing is beautiful and vivid, I want to swim in it. The way she writes enters my dreams and I carry her book with me to read in every spare moment. It's the kind of book you want to slow down because you don't really want it to end. It's an audacious premise, about a woman in ancient times who marries Jesus, and I do love a writer who jumps right into the fire. The way Sue Monk Kidd portrays the story we've heard a million times, from the point of view of Ana, makes it even more heartfelt, and certain parts made me weep.

I know in *The Secret Life of Bees,* Sue Monk Kidd wrote, "She liked to tell everybody that women made the best beekeepers, 'cause they have a special ability built into them to love creatures that sting. It comes from years of loving children and husbands."

I LOVE that she writes about the women that surrounded Jesus when he was on the cross, because really, where were the men? Where were the apostles? I grew up Mormon, and when I heard the Bible stories— I always thought, where are the women? I know they were there, why are they cut out? Why do we only hear the stories of the men? Why are they invisible? *The Book of Longings* makes them visible, and I love this. But the part of the book that I took into my heart was the writings about the Incantation Bowl.

In the beginning of the story, Ana's aunt gives her an Incantation Bowl made of limestone, and tells her that the women scholars in Egypt use them to pray. She says that you draw an image of yourself in the center of the bowl, and then write in a spiral your most secret longing from your deepest heart, your "holy of holies." She says that every day, you run your finger along the spiral of your words and say them aloud and that is your prayer. Ana has many deep desires, and her aunt tells her to choose carefully because it will come true. She finally decides to write, *"Lord our God, hear my prayer, the prayer of my heart. Bless the largeness inside me, no matter how I fear it. Bless my reed pens and my inks. Bless the words I write. May they be beautiful in your sight. May they be visible to eyes not yet born. When I am dust, sing these words over my bones: she was a voice."*

When I read about the Incantation Bowl, it felt familiar, like I had learned about them before. It's quite possible. I studied religion when I attended UCLA, and I had to observe and write my reflections on a religion outside my own. I chose to attend a Goddess Ritual, run by my friend and fellow belly dancer, Laura Kali Shakti, a High Priestess in the Dianic Tradition. I loved the experience of passing the Talking Stick, Casting a Circle, Calling up the Four Corners, and learning about the phases of the moon and how to direct energy in harmony with the cycles of the earth. I ended up gathering a close group of friends and we studied with Laura weekly for the next two years. It's quite possible I learned about the Incantation Bowl during this time.

Incantation Bowls have been used since ancient times to protect, manifest, and make magic. Thousands of Incantation Bowls have been dug up in archaeological finds, and they are a fascinating part of ancient culture.

In any case, when I read *The Book of Longings*, I longed for my own Incantation Bowl. I finished the book a few days before the Super Flower Moon last week, and I decided the timing was perfect.

I've had a supremely difficult couple of years, losing my father to cancer, my marriage to affairs, and my best friend to suicide. My divorce finalized in February and quarantine started in March, so...at this point I need all the help I can get.

I thought about where I could find the perfect bowl during quarantine, and then I realized I already had it. Like Glynda said to Dorothy, "You had the power all along."

Back in 1999, I went on a belly dance safari to Africa. I spent ten glorious days dancing on Mount Kilimanjaro while elephants thundered below, watching giraffes float by, looking at more stars than I could count. I kept a small journal while I was there and I wrote about how my love for Kim, my best friend, was boundless, timeless, eternal, unbreakable. Africa was magic for me. I bought a beautiful rosewood bowl somewhere along the way and I remember picking it up and inhaling the smell of the rosewood. I thought the bowl was so beautiful that I carried it around with me for twenty-one years.

My ex-husband hated it, and refused to let me use it in the house because he didn't like the smell of the rosewood. So now he's gone, and the kids and I have been using the bowl nightly for salads.

But now, the bowl has a new purpose, a perfect purpose, probably what it was meant for all along. After finishing the book, I padded downstairs barefoot in my long nightgown. I pulled the bowl out and walked outside to lay it under the full moon.

I told the kids I'm bathing the bowl in moonlight, and my daughter said," Oh great! Do you realize how crazy you sound? Bathing your bowl?"

(But then today, a few days later, she said, "Mom, do you know what manifesting is? I'm going to manifest my dreams.")

So, back to the bowl. I could think of a hundred sentences for my bowl, but I couldn't pare them down to one beautiful sentence that would encapsulate my innermost secret dreams.

But the search for the sentence was paralyzing me, so I finally took a gold paint pen and just started writing random words that came to me, my own prayer to Sophia, in a spiral. I included the names of my beloveds, and I wrote down every word I could think of that I wanted to make sure was center stage in my life, words like love, light, laughter, moonlight, magic, generosity, abundance, kindness, open heart, open arms, open mind, writing, art, creativity, and Sat Chit Ananda, which means Being, Rapture, Bliss in Sanskrit. I learned the Sat Chit Ananda words from reading Joseph Campbell, and while at Harvard, I did a ritual with my dear friend, Courtney, who wanted to make some changes in her life. Courtney was born and raised in Southern California and had never left. After the ritual, she packed up her car and moved to Alaska. She got a job at the local brewery, met her current husband, and now has two sons and is living out her dream.

So, maybe Sat Chit Ananda will work for me.

In any case, my bowl is gorgeous and I love it. The act of making it brought me such deep joy. With my love of sparkle, I did find it necessary to pour golden glitter into the bowl. I know in Japanese culture, they mend broken bowls with liquid gold, and the bowls are even more beautiful than when they weren't broken. Maybe that will be the same for me.

I told my dear friend, Dolphina, about the Incantation Bowl, and how I felt compelled to help others make their own bowls along with a moving belly dance meditation. She loved the idea, so now she has assigned her goddess book club to read *The Book of Longings*, and I am going to guide them in a ritual on the next full moon to dance and make their own Incantation Bowls.

I love my bowl, and even if it doesn't bring me my wishes, the act of making it was magical on its own. And now I have a physical manifestation of my heart, and each day I trace the golden spiral of words with my finger and say them out loud.

Chapter 43
Make Your Own Declaration of Independence and Plan an Epic Divorce Party

So you had a wedding and declared your devotion to your ex in front of the world. You became a *We*.

Things didn't quite turn out as planned.

Now *We* is back to *I*, and an *I* that is fabulous, wiser, and deserving of a stunning gown and a commitment ceremony — a commitment to a future of being treated like a queen.

I will plan a commitment ceremony when quarantine is over, but I wanted to have one right away, so I bought myself a gorgeous ring, put on my fairy tale gown, and climbed into my favorite place with a glass of champagne — my bathtub, and made the following vows:

I promise myself that I will *never ever* allow myself to be treated poorly again.

I promise to honor my heart and accept only honesty, loyalty, and integrity.

I am forever free of the tyranny of someone else controlling my money and I will handle my own finances with wisdom.

I promise to cherish my soul forever, and make decisions that are for my highest good.

I now walk the Queen's Path, and will never tolerate disrespect again.

I now pronounce me, a Darling Divorce Diva!

Some Divorce Party Ideas:

1. Go to Cabo with your best girlfriends and eat nachos and drink margaritas by the sea.

2. Buy yourself the most beautiful gown you can find, a matching crown, and then invite your people to join you as you declare to the world that you are committed to your future as a queen.

3. Invite your sisters to meet you in NYC for some theater, amazing food and a shopping spree!

4. Take your kids skiing and surprise them with a horse and sleigh ride. While out on the snow, tell them your commitment/declaration and slip a ring on your finger, maybe even a ring for them too, a symbol of your undying devotion to them.

5. Write your Own Declaration of Independence on a scroll and read it aloud. Extra Points if you wear a tri-cornered hat with a big plume and a pair of knickers while you do so. If you can get some friends to shout Huzzah! Back at you after every few sentences, do it.

Chapter 44
The Road To Wealth Is Paved With…
Hula Hoops?

My motto has always been: "Take care of the luxuries, the necessities will take care of themselves." (Thank you Dorothy Parker, for writing this brilliant motto.)

Whether this has served me well or not is a matter of opinion. I have yet to win any financial acumen awards—yet the necessities do seem to take care of themselves and the luxuries... well my definition of luxury changes often. For example, in my 20s, luxury meant traveling the world as what I like to call a "poverty jetsetter." Highlights of my jetsetting days include playing my harmonica for food in Greece, sleeping on bus station floors in Italy, being awakened before dawn by sprinklers while sleeping in the grass in Spain and missing the running of the bulls because I chose the wrong time to brush my teeth. I bought a disposable camera to record my safari to Africa and while National Geographic will most definitely not be contacting me for my shots of lions in the grass, I had an unforgettable time.

Taking care of the luxuries without a steady job has been quite an adventure for me. I will confess that in my quest for prosperity (which keeps eluding me) I have done some rather odd jobs. Let's see, there was the time I was hired to be a flower child at a BelAir mansion garden party where Crosby Stills and Nash were playing in the backyard and I decided it would be a good idea if I was a "real" flower child and took magic mushrooms before going to work. Excellent idea. Flowers were growing and shrinking, all the plastic surgery on the guests was dripping down their faces and I got stuck in a room of cream puffs for over an hour. And then there were all the years of belly dancing, circus shows, and the daily trips to Vegas for an academy award-winning director with a gambling problem.

And then there was the time I was called to see if I knew a professional hula hooper. "I sure do! ME!" I blurted before really thinking. My rent was due. The party booker was surprised and said he would drop by later that afternoon to have me sign a contract. I went directly to the toy store and bought two lime green hula-hoops. I was trying to renew my childhood hula-hoop skills when he knocked on my Royal Palace door. (You know you have a rich fantasy life when you call your battered duplex the Royal Palace.) "So," he said, "Can I see some of your moves?" "Sure," I answered, as I maneuvered the hula-hoops behind my back and tore the tags off so he wouldn't see I had just bought them. Now, I can do some basic hula-hooping but not a whole lot more than the average seven-year-old. I put both hoops on my hips at the same time, a rather impressive trick to those who don't know how to hula-hoop, but simple to those of us hula hooping experts, and spun them around while telling the booker I couldn't show him my *real* tricks because there just wasn't enough room in my living room. He fell for my blatant lies and left. I must confess I felt terribly guilty, lying about my hula-hooping skills, but I was determined to make my rent. This would do the trick.

I had no idea what a professional hula-hooper might do, and as You Tube wasn't even a sparkle in it's inventor's eye, I spent the rest of the day trying to invent some tricks. I spun those damn things on my hips, my feet, my arms, and even my neck, but my windpipe protested that one. The most dazzling trick I invented was spinning one hula-hoop on each arm while bending my head back in a sort of back bend. While it gave me vertigo and I had to lie down whenever I tried it, it would have to do. I dressed up in a 1950's outfit—black pants, white socks, a pink angora sweater–and arrived at the fancy hotel where the party would be held with my hoops in tow. When I walked backstage, a hush fell over the room. I tried to ignore everyone and staked out my own little space. I could hear the other dancers whispering, "The hula-hooper is here! I can't wait to see the hula-hooper!" I felt my face grow hot and wondered what the hell I had gotten myself into, as I laid my hula- hoops on the floor. I figured I better do *something* as they all cleared out of my way, so I acted like I thought a professional athlete would act and started to stretch with a very serious expression on my face. I did a cartwheel over my hoops, touched my toes, did the splits—all the things I learned in Dessa Hepler's backyard acrobatics class when I was eight years old. The party started and I began to panic. I went to a corner and called my best friend. "Kim," I whispered. "SOS. They expect me to do something amazing here. They think I'm a professional hula-hooper. They're relying on me." "Look," she said, always my voice of reason, "it's a corporate party. Most of them can't even do the splits. They'll be impressed with anything you do. Just smile and have fun. They'll love it." "OK, you're right. I'll dazzle them with my illusions of grandeur." I replied, feeling like I might vomit at any moment.

My music started and I glued a big smile on my face and skipped out onto the stage spinning both hula-hoops on each arm. I dropped the hoops and did a few cartwheels through them hoping no one would notice I had no idea what I was doing. It didn't help that the other dancers had all run to the wings, whispering and watching me, waiting for my big tricks. I went for the old performing standby — get Uncle Joe up there onstage and everyone will be so thrilled they won't even watch you. I skipped out into the audience and dragged the big boss onstage. The drunk audience roared with approval and it turned out I was the highlight of the evening (all because the boss did the Robot and the Cabbage Patch, delighting the entire party.) I collected my rent money and went home and into a hot tub, nursing my humiliated, yet triumphant ass.

The next day however, I kept experiencing serious dizzy spells, so bad I would have to grab a wall or sit down. I was convinced I had a brain tumor and it was with a heavy heart that I went to the health clinic between classes at UCLA. In a quiet voice I told the doctor about my spells. I also told her there was a slim possibility the dizziness was caused by the hula-hoop routine I had done the night before. I believed the combination of spinning hoops in my peripheral vision combined with being upside down in a back bend had somehow messed up my equilibrium. The doctor tapped her finger on her chin and said, "I'll be right back." She returned with two other doctors and asked me to repeat the hula-hoop story. They all laughed heartily, which I thought was a bit insensitive considering I might be dying of a brain tumor, but it turned out the dizziness faded after a day or two (as they predicted) and I was fine. I guess it *was* the hula-hoops.

Who knew rent could be paid with hula-hoops? At this stage in my life, however, I've noticed a distinct trend among wealthy people–they all work *really* hard. I think I'm going to try that next. And find a way to take care of the luxuries *and* the necessities. In any case, luxuries for me have changed pretty drastically. In the past, luxuries meant buying velvet capes and evening gowns.

Now I find my most luxurious moments are free.

My best moments this week consisted of watching my daughter sing "Blue Moon" at her school assembly, followed by walking on the beach with my soulful son talking about our potential superpowers (would you rather fly or be invisible or time travel?) as rainbows of light shot out of the sun on both sides like cat whiskers or angel wings or spinning hula hoops, and the dog romped in front of us, his fur the color of a sandcastle. These were moments so exquisite, more precious than anything money could ever buy.

Chapter 45
Magic on the Orient Express

Last year, I turned 50, and my best friend, Kim and I had been planning to do something epic for my half-century birthday. The world was our oyster, and we spent many an hour talking about making our travel dreams come true for my birthday.

And then my world turned upside down. I lost my father, my marriage, and Kim. The kids and I were devastated by the deaths of our beloveds and the searing divorce. Reeling with grief, we needed something bright on the horizon. I didn't know what to do or how to make it through the thick swamp of grief, but I knew I loved to travel and I adore planning a trip. When the kids were little and we'd go to Disney, my ex would say I became a general planning a military strategy, reserving dinner in a castle with a princess, breakfast with a talking bear, and a nighttime boat ride with storytelling pirates. So on my birthday, I created a treasure hunt for my kids and at the end, they found tickets (handmade by me) along with the book, *Murder on the Orient Express*. They screamed and jumped up and down and threw their arms around each other and me. As the mother of teenagers, I like to consider myself a matador, able to handle their wild charging emotions with the swirl of a scarf and the tip of my hat. At least that's how it is in my mind. Planning an epic trip gave us months of swirling scarves, as we spent many mealtimes talking about what wondrous things we would experience together. Here's part of what I planned:

1. Venice, Italy to visit the atelier of my dream costume maker, Antonia Sautter, along with the Guggenheim and seeing an opera.

2. One glorious indulgent night taking my dream vintage train, the Orient Express, now called the Venice-Simplon-Orient-Express, through the Alps to Paris.

3. Paris to see my favorite bookshop: Shakespeare and Co., the Van Gogh paintings made of light so it feels like you are INSIDE the paintings, and I wanted to put my arms around the kids and watch the Eiffel Tower glitter while listening to "La Conga Bilicoti" by Josephine Baker.

4. Josephine Baker's Castle, Chateau Des Milandes, near the Dordogne River.

5. Burgundy to see my favorite vineyards.

(I counted all sections of the trip as "work" for me, since I was actually researching for my new mystery novel about the theft of costumes. Except for Burgundy, but that was my own personal research for the best wine to drink after a long day writing!)

But right now, tonight, on this moonlit night, I am dreaming of trains, and specifically the luxury train to end all trains: the Orient Express.

I have always loved the style of the Golden Age of Travel: steamer trunks, hats and gloves, uniformed porters in darling hats carrying my gorgeous luggage, hatboxes, makeup cases, and the interaction that can happen between people thrown together during a trip. And so I decided to create my own Golden Age of Travel with this trip. I couldn't find the perfect luggage-- I had it in my mind that it needed to be pink with a glittering martini glass on the front. Why a martini glass? Partly because I love cocktail style even though I'm not a big drinker, and partly because my first mystery novel is called *Martini Mystery* and my publishing company is called House of Martini, so I guess my love of a beautiful martini glass is evident. I don't even like martinis, but I love martini style: a beautiful glass and the mixing and stirring and care that goes into making the perfect cocktail. So back to my luggage, I finally found the perfect sizes and perfect shades of pink luggage on Amazon-- three suitcases for $100-- seriously. I ordered the beauties and then painted my own martini glass on the front with iridescent gold paint and a dash of glitter, aka fairy dust. I loved the way they looked as we checked them, packed them, stacked them-- in every instance they were beautiful, especially when sitting next to my hatboxes.

One of my favorite parts of the train trip was planning our outfits. I love vintage fashion and I have an entire closet full of vintage style dresses, hats, purses, gloves, and shoes. The kids and I had a ball planning their travel ensembles, shopping at my favorite shop in Salem, Modern Millie. And we found some fabulous flapper hats and a bowler for Henry at the fabulous steampunk shop in Salem, Emporium 52. When I lived in New Orleans, I had bought some spectacular hats at a shop in the French Quarter called Fleur De Paris. We devoted one entire suitcase just for the train, and carried two hatboxes full of hats, careful not to let the jaunty luscious plumes get smashed.

You can imagine that for a mystery writer who loves glamorous travel style, the first place they are going to head is straight to the Orient Express. Made famous in Agatha Christie's brilliant mystery, *Murder on the Orient Express*, the train is legendary for its inspirational style, attracting artists, movie stars, filmmakers, and writers for more than a century. The storied train started rolling back in 1883, and passengers might see Tolstoy, Mata Hari, Marlene Dietrich, James Bond or even Dracula riding along with them.

On the morning of our train ride, we put on our outfits and caused quite a stir in the lobby of our hotel in Venice, The Bauer, waiting to be picked up for our trip. Part of the Orient Express service is picking you up at your hotel in a gorgeous wooden boat. When the beautiful boat arrived with its gleaming wood, we all boarded and the bellhops tagged our luggage. With the warm wind ruffling our plumes and the light reflecting off the water, we were immediately swept into our own personal movie of sumptuous glamour and glitz.

When we arrived at the station, we all walked to the train, and the kids quickly realized we were the only ones dressed up. "Mom!" They admonished me. "Why are we the only ones dressed up?" I shrugged as people all around us asked to take our pictures. This was another case of Marci Darling daydreaming about style for a particular event, and thinking everyone else would be thinking the same thing, and finding out once we were there that no one else was actually thinking about dressing up at all. Like the time I had us all wear fairy wings to a *Midsummer Night's Dream* production in the woods, because I had somehow gotten it into my head that everyone would be dressed as fairies. They weren't. My kids are used to showing up to events overdressed, and I always tell them it's better to be overdressed than underdressed. I'm not sure they agree, but it is what it is. They will have lots of stories when they grow up about their daydreaming mother. In any case, everyone at the train station seemed to be delighted by our quirky ensembles, and we posed for many photos in between the kids glaring at me.

The Orient Express is known for its stunning detail, and it didn't disappoint. An elegant tea and snacks were set up in our cars. We were assigned an adorable porter who was wearing a crisp blue uniform, just like my Golden Age fantasy. We opened the door between our two cars, watching the Alps go by outside our windows. Shades of green, fields of wildflowers, waterfalls... I had bought the kids leather journals in Venice, and I gave them pens and told them to write what they were seeing.

We had a fancy formal lunch with sparkling silver, white napkins, and tiny teacups lined with shimmering gold. Then we returned to our cars to watch the mountains, well the kids did. I stopped on the way back to have a long talk with a very lovely woman I had just met. She was wearing white, tall and elegant, and something about the experience of being on the train together created an instant bond. I shared with her my grief, my fears, how lost I felt, and how we were all in a dream-state, mourning our massive losses. She shared with me her own heartbreak and soaring career, as I told her about my lack of paying career due to being a stay-at-home mom for 16 years. She assured me something magical was going to happen for me, and I so wanted to believe her. I returned to our car to rest and talk to the kids, before getting ready in our formal wear for our five-course dinner, with a chef so talented, my vegetable-hating son ate his entire plate proclaiming it was the "best asparagus he ever had." We were assigned the "Lalique" car, which is a gorgeous french luxury crystal and glass style of decor.

Again, there was something incredibly magical about being on the exquisite train with the teenagers. We talked, we acted fancy, sipping our tea with our pinkies in the air, napkins in our lap, no elbows on the table. After dinner, we went to the raucous cocktail car where a pianist played jazz. The kids were half asleep at that point, which I discovered when I turned around and they were all laying sideways on their chairs with glassy eyes. Teenagers are funny, sometimes they are so grown-up, and sometimes they are like toddlers, clutching teddy bears and rubbing their eyes. When we returned to our rooms, we found our porter had flipped the plush couches into beds and set out pajamas and slippers. On my way back, I met my elegant friend eating dinner solo so I sat with her for a while and we talked. I knew all about her life, but I didn't know her last name, and when I finally asked her name, it turns out she's the head of a huge filmmaking company. She was traveling between film sets and on her way to a movie premiere in London. Glamorous indeed.

We fell asleep that night watching *Top Hat* with Fred Astaire and Ginger Rogers, as the train rumbled along, rocking us with its rumbling. The next morning we arrived in Paris... but that's a different story.

It's been a year since our trip, and the kids light up when we talk about it. They talk about the coziness of the train, the lightning outside the window, and how they will never forget it. There were no murders on this particular train ride, but there was magic, and memories we will carry with us for the rest of our lives, like a pocket full of gold.

Chapter 46
Speeding Into Magic: When Something Terrible Becomes Something Wonderful

Magic appears in the most unusual packages. While these packages are rarely delivered to your front door, they tend to arrive in unexpected ways once you leave your comfort zone. I consider myself a bit of a master of magic because it has permeated my life in ways I never expected, and here is what I have found: magic lies in motion; magic happens when you ask for something and allow the other person to say no (a well-kept secret-- they usually say yes!); for magic to happen you absolutely have to believe in the unbelievable; and magic always follows those who appreciate that the glass is half full.

For example, when I was 23 years old and living in Los Angeles, I drove my beat-up old VW bug home from work one evening. I had experienced a particularly rough night and in an effort to make myself feel better, I was driving along the ocean, barefoot and blasting the radio. When I saw the red lights flashing in my rear view mirror, my heart sank. And to make matters worse, as the cop came up to my window, my need to weep came out as a snorting burst of laughter that wouldn't stop, one of those horrible cases of guffaws where the harder you try to stop, the harder the giggles keep coming. Not only was I forced to take several drunk tests, even though I hadn't had one drink, but my tormentors gave me a $250 speeding ticket. Talk about raining on my parade! That was more money than I made in a week. But I was determined to keep my chin up and find the positive part of the nightmare. I went to court and asked the judge for community service instead of paying the fine. He sent me to the United Way. In those days you weren't automatically assigned to pick up trash in a dayglo jumpsuit. You were sent to a volunteer coordinator who talked to you, found out your interests and assigned you to a suitable place. I had a long talk with a little old man behind a dingy gray desk, his nose pinched from too-tight glasses. He thumbed through a box of index card (ah yes, pre-computer days) as I told him about my many interests. He assigned me to answer phones at a non-profit theater called The Globe in West Hollywood.

The Globe was owned by a large man named Thad, a merchant marine with a ponytail who was obsessed with Shakespeare and had built an exact half-size replica of the original Globe Theater in England. *Midsummer Night's Dream* was playing, my favorite Shakespearean play, and as luck would have it (lucky for me, not her), one of the fairies hurt her back. Thad suggested to the director that I replace her and they called me in for a little audition. Yes, I said eagerly, I can do everything the previous fairy(a professional gymnast and stuntwoman) did — well, ok, I can't do a back flip, but I can do a somersault. And no, I can't do a front handspring, but I can touch my toes. And as for sliding headfirst down a thick rope hung from the ceiling, um, sure, I'll give it a whirl! My heart pounded as I wrapped the rope around my foot and hung upside down. I mean, how hard could this be? The other fairy did it every night and she hadn't broken anything. On second thought, she had broken something — her back! But too late, I was already hanging. Well, just grip the rope tightly, I told myself and at least you won't fall. I closed my eyes and went for it. The rope swung wildly and all the other fairies had to jump out of the way.

It reminded me of the time I had set about 100 feet of rope on a lift chair when I worked as a ski lift operator at Robert Redford's ski resort, Sundance, in Utah. It nearly broke the entire lift by getting entangled in the chair, the cables, and the trees. I watched it go down the mountain, knocking snow off the trees, which caused the lift to bounce and shake. I ran back inside my cozy little hut and tried to appear nonchalant should anyone come looking for the fool that had sent a rope down alone. That's when I was radioed that Robert Redford was on his way up the mountain. I ran outside with a large shovel, hoping to impress him with my hard work. I shoveled so intently, I didn't pay attention to the lift chairs and got knocked in the head hard enough to force me to lie down in the snow. When Mr. Redford reached the top of the lift, he was greeted with the sight of his hardworking lift operator lying down, holding her noggin. "Are you alright?" he kindly asked me. "Oh yeah," I answered, raising one puffy parka arm in the air. "I'm fine, just resting for a minute, enjoying the snow."

Back to the Globe. So here I was, in a similar humiliating situation involving ropes and bumps on the head. Hanging upside down in the middle of a stage covered in rope burns while a group of professional actors and stunt people stood in the wings, covering their own heads, I proceeded to do what I always do in these types of situations (which I'm afraid I get into rather often). I pretended everything was just fine. I flipped off the end of the rope, smiled, and said "ta-da!" Much to my amazement (and everyone else's) I got the part. Other than the physical impossibilities, my experience in the play was incomparable. Many of the cast members became lifelong friends. I got to listen to the Bard's ingenious words every night. I got to meet Mikhail Baryshnikov, a personal idol of mine (he was friends with Puck), and I met my best friend and soul mate, Kim, who played the fairy, Cobweb. Best of all, I paid off my speeding ticket by performing. Who knew that a speeding ticket would forever change my life for the better? Who knew that I was speeding right into magic that night? Which makes me wonder, what magic is around the corner for me now? Divorce is much worse than a speeding ticket, so I can't even imagine what wondrous event is about to appear. I'll keep you posted.

Monkey Business

(New Traditional Christmas Carol sung to the tune of
Christmas is Coming, The Goose Is Getting Fat)

Christmas is coming, my ex is getting rude
Holiday expenses put him in a bad mood.

Divorce sucks, okay, but I'm singing fa-la-la.
Holidays are awesome when there are no in-laws.

No more fighting or criticizing me
Haul out the vodka, it's time for a martini!

Setting up the tree solo is hard, but never fear,
I'm just glad something is hard around here.
(Just kidding, everything is hard.)

 I pull out the wedding bells, it doesn't really matter
I smile to myself as I watch them shatter.

Here's the ornament we bought while in Vermont.
Oopsy! Sip! Stomp! Stomp! Stomp!

So even in divorce there is a bright side.
No more In-laws! Just peace and love and light.

Acknowledgements

I'd like to thank Professor Pain for coming in, uninvited, lighting a match, and burning it all down. Thank you Professor Pain, for teaching me what it means to rise. I'd also like to thank my Martini Club who are always cheering for me and pointing me towards the light, even when I can't see it. Thank you to my sisters, who I know will take me in should I show up on their doorstep one day in a basket looking for a soft place to lay my head. Thank you to Ashley Longshore for showing me how to follow my own path, no matter how crazy. Thank you to my ex, not for the pain, but for all the wonderful parts, the Busby Berkeley Dreams, that I have put into a steamer trunk and buried, so I can dig them up later when it all doesn't hurt so much. Thank you to Kim who showed me what it means to love. Thank you to Annabelle and Henry, my hearts.

About Miss Marci Darling

Marci Darling is a sassy bon vivant whose previous careers include belly dancer, burlesque dancer, showgirl, circus acrobat, and preschool teacher. She has performed around the world and danced on tour with The Go-Go's, the B-52's, Placido Domingo and Paul McCartney. She is the author of two mystery novels: *Martini Mystery: A Love Letter to New Orleans* and *The Champagne Scandal: The Spirits Are Calling*. She is known around her house as MOM, or the Monarch of Merriment. She holds a Masters degree from Harvard, a BA from UCLA in Creative Writing, and a Certificate in Novel Writing from Stanford. She currently lives near the sea in a little New England town with her two teenagers, two dogs and three cats.

You can read more of her writings at www.marcidarling.com

Made in the USA
Coppell, TX
04 January 2021

47591159R00115